DEMONETISATION AND BLACK MONEY

DEMONETISATION AND BLACK MONEY

C. Rammanohar Reddy

with a foreword by

Y. V. Reddy

Orient BlackSwan

DEMONETISATION AND BLACK MONEY

ORIENT BLACKSWAN PRIVATE LIMITED

Registered Office
3-6-752 Himayatnagar, Hyderabad 500 029 (Telangana), India
e-mail: centraloffice@orientblackswan.com

Other Offices
Bengaluru, Bhopal, Chennai, Guwahati, Hyderabad, Jaipur, Kolkata, Lucknow, Mumbai, New Delhi, Noida, Patna, Vijayawada

ISBN 978-93-86392-61-9

025196

27022017

Typeset in
ITC Berkeley Oldstyle Std 11/14.4
by Le Studio Graphique, Gurgaon 122 001

Printed in India at
Yash Printographics, Delhi

Published by
Orient Blackswan Private Limited
3-6-752, Himayatnagar, Hyderabad 500 029
e-mail: info@orientblackswan.com

Contents

SECTION II

SECTION III

SECTION IV

Tables

ABBREVIATIONS

ADB	Asian Development Bank
ADR	Association for Democratic Reforms
ATM	Automated Teller Machine
BIS	Bank of International Settlements
BJP	Bharatiya Janata Party
BNPMIPL	Bank Note Paper Mill Private Limited
BoP	Balance of Payments
BRBNMPL	Bharatiya Reserve Bank Note Mudran Private Limited
CBDT	Central Board of Direct Taxes
CBLO	Collaterised borrowing and lending obligation
CEC	Chief Election Commissioner
CPI	Communist Party of India
CPI	Corruption Perception Index
CRR	Cash Reserve Ratio
CSO	Central Statistical Office
CTS	Cheque Truncation System
DTAA	Double Taxation Avoidance Agreement
ECB	European Commercial Bank
ECI	Election Commission of India
ECS	Electronic Clearing Service
EMU	European Monetary Union
EU	European Union
FIIs	Foreign Institutional Investors
FY	Financial Year
GDP	Gross Domestic Product

GNP	Gross National Product
GoI	Government of India
GST	Goods and Services Tax
GVA	Gross Value Added
IDS	Income Declaration Scheme
IMF	International Monetary Fund
IMPS	Immediate Payment Service
IT	Income Tax
JAM	Jan Dhan Aadhaar Mobile
MGNREGS	Mahatma Gandhi National Rural Employment Guarantee Scheme
MICR	Magnetic Ink Character Recognition
MMTC	Metals and Minerals Corporation of India
MPs	Members of Parliament
MSME	Micro, Small and Medium Enterprises
MSS	Market Stabilisation Scheme
NACH	National Automated Clearing House
NAS	National Accounting System
NCEUS	National Commission for Employment in the Unorganised Sector
NDA	National Democratic Alliance
NEFT	National Electronic Funds Transfer
NGO	Non-governmental organisation
NIPFP	National Institute of Public Finance and Policy
NPCI	National Payments Corporation of India
NREGA	National Rural Employment Guarantee Act
NSSO	National Sample Survey Office
PMGKY	Pradhan Mantri Garib Kalyan Yojana
PNs	Participatory Notes
PoS	Point of Scale
PPIs	Prepaid Payment Instruments
PPP	Public–Private Partnership
PTE	Pure tax evasion

PWC	Pricewaterhousecoopers
RBI	Reserve Bank of India
RGTS	Real Time Gross Settlement
SIFMIs	Systematically Important Financial Market Infrastructures
SIT	Special Investigation Team
SPMCIL	Security Printing and Mining Corporation of India Limited
UPI	Unified Payment Interface
USSD	Unstructured Supplementary Service Data
VDIS	Voluntary Disclosure of Income Scheme
VDS	Voluntary Disclosure Scheme
WPI	Wholesale Price Index

Foreword

Demonetisation 2016 was undoubtedly a historic and unprecedented event. There has perhaps been no other policy decision that has affected the lives of a billion people directly and all at once. The disruption in a wide range of normal economic activities on a mass scale has lasted for a longer duration than any other disruptive event in peacetime. It is difficult to find a parallel in terms of the range of economic activities that have been hit by an economic policy decision.

Never before has a central bank been required to produce currency notes in such large quantities at such incredibly short notice and make it available to millions of people spread over vast territories with diverse transportation challenges. Collection of and accounting for returned notes deposited in banks has been even more challenging. The conduct of elections could be a good parallel in India to the scale of Demonetisation 2016, but in the latter case the central bank did not have the luxury of adequate notice. It is indeed impressive that the whole banking system dedicated itself for several days to implement the decision.

It is no wonder the announcement of Demonetisation 2016 was made by none other than the head of the government, Narendra Modi, the Prime Minister of India, which is indeed a rare occurrence. Demonetisation 2016 deserves to be considered a historic event for breaking many records, but there is another reason as well.

For millions, a majority of our population, Demonetisation 2016 led to a virtual denial of freedom of movement, drying up of sources of livelihood and deprivation for no fault of theirs. Yet, people at large did not revolt. They went through not just inconvenience, but pain. While the agony was palpable, the patience of the masses was beyond belief. There was a silent but eloquent demonstration of some deep, shared intense feeling. That feeling, I believe, is one of disgust with the state of affairs in recent years, and a belief that this may be the only way in which they could express it.

The question that baffles some of us is: what is the disgust about? Is it about counterfeit currency? Is it about terrorist financing? Is it about black money?

Or is it about corruption, one of the driver of black money? The masses are the victims of corruption when they try to access even basic public services, while the corrupt accumulate black money by demanding payment for public services of all kinds. The masses also have no avenues to protest against corruption; they are even afraid of the consequences of protesting. Was this silently expressed disgust then about corruption?

The intense but silent feelings the masses expressed could even have been a protest against inequality. It may also have been a hope that there would be one-time material benefits. Could it have been a hope that the promise of Prime Minister Modi that there would be cleansing of patently unfair governance would be fulfilled?

While the behaviour of the masses was bewildering, equally unfathomable were the intentions behind or the purpose of Demonetisation 2016, an exercise which, though it had mass appeal,also had on the face of it stupendous downside risks and uncertain benefits. In other words, the decision to go ahead with Demonetisation 2016 might not have been the result of calculated risk taking, but may have been taken out of inspiration or political instinct. It could have even been aimed at creating a behavioural change towards black money.

Prime Minister Modi obviously had the confidence that the masses would be supportive of the decision on Demonetisation 2016. The fact that the government, under his leadership, had earlier taken a series of unprecedented policy measures relating to black money lends credibility to his intentions. Perhaps the changing narratives have sustained the faith of the people in the operation. In any case, Demonetisation 2016 is unlikely to be the end, but actually the beginning of the story.

Demonetisation 2016 has unsurprisingly become a matter of intense and contentious debate. It is hailed and condemned by different camps with equal vehemence. It invites comments from academia, policymakers and analysts globally. It is such a rare and unusual event that the debate was and, perhaps, still is less than well informed.

Rammanohar Reddy's book is an invaluable contribution to a good understanding of this complex story, a story which started abruptly and is still unfolding. My friend, Ram, with his vast and rich experience built on professional expertise in both economics and journalism, provides in a nutshell conceptual clarity and global experience as a backdrop to facts and perceptions surrounding Demonetisation 2016. The narration provides detail but keeps its focus on the broader objectives of Demonetisation 2016.

Having presented what has been and what should have been, Ram, wisely ends the volume with a chapter titled 'What Next?' I believe that our economic system is ripe for a change, and Demonetisation 2016 has triggered the possibility of a change not because of the questionable decision, but because of the nature of the reactions of the masses to the enigmatic decision of Prime Minister Modi.

I believe that an invisible non-quantifiable message from the people's response to the crisis is actually an implicit mandate for the authorities as well as for society as a whole.

Is it that the masses demand a change in the way the government and the more well-to-do who deal with the government conduct themselves? Are the masses demanding a less unfair and more effective standard of governance? In any case, it is an opportunity to introspect.

The most obvious objective of demonetisation is the elimination of the stock of counterfeit currency. However, Ram refers to our dependence on imports for manufacture of currency. Can this make India more vulnerable to infusion of counterfeit currency? Why could we not become self-sufficient on inputs for manufacture of currency? Is it due to lack of expertise, technology, raw material or other reasons? Is it possible that our security features are not invincible, which they should be? How do our investigative methods and incentive systems deal with counterfeiting, compared with other large-sized economies, say China?

Black money in the form of cash was the target of the Demonetisation 2016 exercise. Cash, by itself, is neither black nor white, but the cash with a bearer who cannot explain it in terms of taxes paid could be characterised as black money. All cash or currency in circulation originates in the banking system. Information should be readily available about the bank's branches and withdrawal of cash. The information about accounts which have seen withdrawal of cash of large magnitudes should be readily available, and on a continuing basis. Has this information been sought or used in the past to trace the origins of large cash-based transactions? Some years ago, a cash withdrawal tax was levied and later withdrawn. The government should have information in its possession through the tax department itself on large cash withdrawals. How many of such known cases were probed and matched with income tax returns filed? If not, why has this not been done?

More generally, are there systems that encourage tax authorities to utilise the information other than what has been filed by the assessee? The 'scrutiny' and 'probe' of assessees' income is generally on the basis of information provided by them. The major source of black money is out of transactions not declared to the authorities. To what extent is the government using technology and information that is available in ordinary course of business for its scrutiny and assessment of individual tax returns of high net worth individuals?

The sources and uses of black money through the financial system have been increasing and, perhaps, have overtaken those in cash. Black money through the financial system may remain within the domestic economy, or may be going out of the country and being brought back. Are there incentives that facilitate such transactions? No doubt, the recent review of bilateral treaties is a bold and welcome step. But should other aspects of incentives for round-tripping such as the role of participatory notes be addressed? Round-tripping requires the collusion of banks and associated institutions with a cross border presence. Have their roles been assessed?

The use of the financial system for generating and using black money requires creation of legal entities like shell companies. That would be possible only with the aid of company secretaries and chartered accountants. Have we assessed whether the functioning of self-regulatory bodies, which are integral to standards of governance, is responsible for creation of black money?

Tobin Tax, a tax on financial transactions especially on cross-border flows, has been advocated on several grounds, and one of them has been the information that it provides to the tax administration. The tax could be nominal and, in any case, the cost of administering and compliance may not be high. Is it now time for us to review the position we had taken on this in the past?

Our post-Independence experience should be instructive. What was the single most important source of black money in the first 50 years after our independence? It was gold smuggling that provided an unofficial market in foreign exchange and in domestic gold trade. It was inappropriate, and indeed an indefensible restriction which made the culture of non-compliance widely prevalent across all sections. This law hurt us and our economy. Are some of our laws and not the citizens the cause of black money?

We had a draconian law called the Foreign Exchange Regulation Act. What was our experience with administering such a law, if that was in reality administered at all? Is there need to review what a government can and should do in economic matters?

Have we learnt our lessons from the laws that hurt us in the past? Two recent examples may be in order. A law has been passed by the Lok Sabha in regard to demonetised currency notes. A person having possession of such notes beyond a minimum is liable for punishment with a fine and imprisonment. What purpose does it serve and at what cost? Presumably, after demonetisation, the old currency is not even legal tender and so it is a scrap of paper, a relic of the past. If someone uses it to get wrongful loss or gain, it is a case of merely cheating the gullible. Should we be giving greater attention to counterfeiting and indigenisation of manufacturing currency?

More than 50 years ago, we had rationing in Chennai (then called Madras), and there was no legal way of having a dinner for guests since no free market for grain existed. The wedding cards contained a sentence,'Guests are requested to bring their own rations.' Technically, guests were supposed to get grain which was pooled and cooked for the guests themselves. But in reality, no guest ever had to bring grain. Is it possible that the recent proposal to have a law prescribing a ceiling on expenditure at weddings is somewhat similar?

It is obvious that public policymakers should remind themselves of the saying, 'Physician, heal thyself'. Cleansing the system of the ills of the past requires fundamental changes in both the government and governed, not merely action against the governed suspected of being guilty. How should the change in public policy be considered, taking account of our experience so far?

First, many of us have been assuming that markets are bad or unfair (market failures) and so the state (government) should perform the functions. But we have realised that the state (government) also can also fail (state failures). So, it is necessary to consider the sectors or activities that are best suited for markets to function and those that are best suited for the state to function. The state should certainly give priority to those activities which the private sector cannot provide (law and order; police, judiciary).

Second, the state and the market do not operate in isolation or in separate compartments. They interact and their effectiveness as well as efficiency will depend on the nature of such a relationship. Public policy itself influences relative efficiency by determining the nature of the relationship between the public and private sectors.

Third, governments are keen to pursue business friendly policies. This often leads to being friendly to select business houses, often bordering on crony capitalism. Governments have to move towards being market friendly, which means encouraging competition and appropriate regulation. Experience shows that regulators may also be captured by the interests of the regulated. How do we structure the role of the state and the market depending on the sector and industry?

Fourth, states in India are competing to excel in 'Ease of Doing Business'. Should we not also have a 'Ease of Living Index' which measures the ease with which a citizen can access services from the government from birth to death, from receiving a birth certificate to the family receiving a death certificate?

Fifth, what should be the balance between incentives and disincentives (punishments) in the design in order to minimise generation of black money?

Sixth, has the prescription of punishment by itself been effective? What has been the probability of being caught while doing wrong, and then investigated, prosecuted and punishment effectuated? Is it possible that for a rational person, the possibility of being punished is rather remote, relative to most other countries?

Finally, we are aware that the discharge of any responsibility assigned to government requires resources to perform the necessary functions. There are competing demands for resources, for the public sector as a whole and for administering the law in specific cases. Spreading the resources thinly makes all interventions too meek or weak and ineffective.

These are but a few of the many questions that need to be posed to determine the way forward.

Prime Minister Modi struck a chord with the masses during the pain of demonetisation, and perhaps even after. The masses still place faith in him that he will deliver what he promised. But they will not wait for long. There is a lurking fear that Demonetisation 2016 may turn out to be a non-event; except for bitter memories of pain. Many of us hoping to see Demonetisation 2016 as a game changer would also be disillusioned.

I am delighted to write a foreword for this deeply relevant book. Rammanohar Reddy should be congratulated for bringing out a book that sets out an analysis of the concepts, decisions, the course of events and the impact of Demonetisation 2016. It is not only eloquent on the anguish but also provides a trigger for a less ill-informed and more productive discussion. The book, I believe, will lead to an informed debate on the changes that are needed in the days and months ahead.

Hyderabad
February 2017

Y. V. REDDY

Preface

For Indians, 8 November 2016 started out no different from any other day. The first hint that it would be somewhat unusual came around 7.30 pm when announcements started flashing on the TV asking viewers to stand by for an important announcement by the Prime Minister. When the Prime Minister did appear and announced demonetisation, everyone recognised that it was more than just an important announcement. It was earth-shattering news that was, according to subsequent rumours, news even to many in the Union cabinet. It easily must have been one of the best-kept secrets in the history of the Republic of India.

The days after the announcement saw an explosion of analyses and comments on demonetisation, black money and counterfeit currency. However, it seemed to me that the public debate, voluble and rich as it was, did not quite engage with the issues in their entirety and complexity. This book aims to do just that; it presents the larger picture by thinking through the wider aspects of demonetisation and black money.

It must be pointed out that this book is neither a research-based piece of academic work nor is it a journalistic analysis. It is an attempt, at short notice, to first clarify and then analyse this immensely complex subject.

There are three strands running through this slim volume. The first one is an explanation and analysis of Demonetisation 2016, the nature of black money, the links of 'notebandi' with black money and the effect this major event had on the people of India. The second strand is a discussion of what could have been done differently, causing less disruption to the economy and minimising the hardship to citizens. The third strand is an examination of new objectives like digitalisation that have emerged after the announcement, followed by questions about where we are now and what the agenda on dealing with black money should really be.

The book has been organised around 14 short chapters plus two essays in the beginning and at the end, all of which first lay out and then dissect the important issues. There are also four annexures at the end and three appendices to three of the chapters.

The book has been written for the general reader. So, as far as possible, the use of technical terms has been avoided and an effort has been made to keep the discussion as simple as possible.

The text is fully referenced, but for ease of reading footnotes have been kept to a minimum. For those who may be interested in reading further, there is an extensive bibliography at the end of the book, organised chapter by chapter.

In the end, I would like to mention that this book is the outcome of a journey that I, like millions of other Indians, undertook, trying to understand and then come to terms with the enormity of Demonetisation 2016.

Acknowledgements

The origins of this book lie in a number of conversations I had with Dr Y. V. Reddy, former Governor of the Reserve Bank of India and Chairman of the Fourteenth Finance Commission, soon after 8 November 2016, when the decision on demonetisation was announced. We found ourselves arguing from very different perspectives. It was at that time that the idea of this book took shape.

I cannot say it enough that I owe Dr Reddy an immense debt for guiding this work from conceptualisation to developing the framework and then refining the arguments in each chapter. He kept pointing me in new directions and introduced me to a number of policymakers and commentators who freely gave of their time. He also cast a critical eye on all chapters, not just once but over many revisions. I am also grateful to him for having penned a very interesting foreword to this book.

Dr Reddy's imprint on this work can especially be seen in the four chapters in Section IV: 'Cash, Money and Liquidity', 'Impact on the Banking System', 'Impact on Reserve Bank of India' and 'Demonetisation, Black Money and Gold'.

It is stating the obvious that but for Dr Reddy's involvement this book would not have been written.

Apart from Dr Reddy, a very large number of people helped in writing this book. I would like especially to thank K. S. Ananth, V. Bhaskar, Abhiman Das, Vepa Kamesam, K. S. Kanagasabathy, Aarati Krishnan, C. R. L. Narasimhan, Sriram Panchu, A. Premchand, Dennis Rajakumar, E. Kumar Sharma and

Usha Thorat for their help. Given the nature of the subject and the short time over which this book was prepared, their help was invaluable. Indeed, some of their contributions have been incorporated in this book.

Special thanks to Abhishek Shaw to whom I have to apologise for having commandeered several of his weekends to help me with the research.

I must also acknowledge the help I received from Pinaki Chakraborty, Sunil Nagpal, G. Sreekumar, Ravi Srivastava and Durganand Swamy while preparing the manuscript.

An earlier version of chapter 9 was delivered as a key note 'Missing from Demonetisation: Money in Elections and Politics as Business' on 10 January 2017, at the conference on 'Political Economy of Contemporary India' at the Indira Gandhi Institute of Development Research (IGIDR), Mumbai. Thanks to R. Nagaraj and Sripad Motiram for inviting me to give a key note address on this subject.

At Orient BlackSwan, Mimi Choudhury, Nilanjana Majumdar and Uday Rao believed in this book and took it to press on a priority basis. The involvement and support of Nilanjana was crucial. She also put up with all my demands and requests. Thank you and sorry!

It has been just 10–12 weeks since I started work on the book, but during that time everything else came to a halt. At home 'THE BOOK' had a silent but overpowering presence. I would like to tell Aman and Nandini that I am now back. Thank you both for indulging me during the writing of this book.

Hyderabad
20 February 2017

C. RAMMANOHAR REDDY

Demonetisation 2016

An Unfolding Story

In an address to the nation on the evening of 8 November 2016, Prime Minister Narendra Modi announced that from midnight all Rs 500 and Rs 1,000 currency notes would cease to be legal tender.

The announcement invalidated Rs 14.18 lakh crore (trillion) of currency. At one stroke, as much as 86 per cent of the Rs 16.41 lakh crore (trillion) of currency in circulation was deprived of its status as legal tender. Some exceptions were allowed for some time, but the larger impact was of a society emptied of cash.

Banks were to be closed the next day and ATMs too would be shut for a day. When they reopened on 10 November, the public could deposit the Rs 500 and Rs 1,000 notes they had with them in their bank accounts, after going through a process of identification and verification. Individuals and organisations could exchange these old currency notes for new ones as well. They could also draw cash from their bank accounts. Both were subjected to tight limits and as people were to learn over the next six weeks, these limits were continuously changed, causing considerable difficulty.

It was officially revealed much later that the proposal to demonetise the high denomination notes had been contemplated at the highest levels since February 2016, but when it happened it was a bolt from the blue.

The aim was to attack black money and defeat counterfeiting of currency. As the week progressed it was claimed on behalf of the massive currency withdrawal that it would lead to a behavioural change, end the phenomenon of black money in the country and lead to a substantial increase in tax revenue.

The immediate effect, however, was that much of commerce froze. Electronic transactions took place, but in the absence of cash, much of everyday transactions in markets ceased. Institutions and people struggled to adapt—some continued to use the old notes for a while, some resorted to barter, and some entered into credit arrangements.

Demonetisation 2016[1]. It is difficult to recall another economic policy decision by the Government of India (GoI) in recent times that has caused so much shock, upheaval, and disruption. The official narrative is that the pain in the short term will be outweighed by major benefits in the long term.

Yet, three months after Demonetisation 2016, while the long lines outside banks had disappeared, there were no immediate gains to report. Losses in the informal or unorganised sector (where the weak subsisted) were, however, yet to be recouped. Meanwhile, the objectives kept shifting; and it was not clear how much black money had been unearthed or was going to be unearthed. Follow-up actions were also scarce.

Demonetisation 2016 is a story which will continue to unfold well into the future.

---

[1] The term 'demonetisation' was itself never used by the GoI or the Reserve Bank of India. The gazette notification of 8 November making the formal announcement only says that the 'specified bank notes [Rs 500 and Rs 1000 notes] shall cease to be legal tender' (see Annexure II). Since the decision was to demonetise two high denomination currency notes and that is how the action has been understood, this is the term that has been used in this book. 'Demonetisation' has also become part of everyday usage. Other commonly used terms include 'note ban' and, in the north, 'notebandi'.

RATIONALE, DESIGN AND IMPLEMENTATION

In hindsight, we should not have been surprised that such a major decision on black money was taken.

The subject of black money had become a major part of the public discourse over the previous decade. Activists and non-governmental organisations (NGOs) had been frequently raising the issue, the Supreme Court of India had actively intervened, the GoI had issued a White Paper on Black Money in 2012, and political parties had promised more action if elected to office.

The Narendra Modi government was regularly pilloried for not fulfilling what the media claimed were extravagant promises made during the 2014 election campaign. To be fair to the Modi government, it had been taking a number of steps since 2015 to tackle black money in the domestic economy and deal with what had been taken out of the country (see chapter 5). These may have been small measures when compared to what was announced on 8 November 2016, but one should perhaps not have been surprised that the government ended up doing something very dramatic on black money.

A dramatic gesture by the government to send a political message to the voters and to reinvigorate its political base midway through its term is one thing, but the need for clarity on objectives, formulating an effective strategy, and demonstrating sensitivity towards citizens are all another matter.

The Prime Minister's speech on 8 November spoke about demonetisation attacking corruption, black money and counterfeit currency (thereby striking at terrorist financing). The gazette notification on demonetisation the next day left out corruption and stuck to 'unaccounted wealth' and 'fake currency'.

Once banks re-opened, there was chaos. People stood for hours in queues to deposit the cash they had in the demonetised currencies. Others stood for hours in other queues to withdraw cash from their bank accounts. Often banks quickly ran out of cash to disburse. There was simply not enough to go round and ATMs had not been calibrated to handle the new currency notes. That was the first sign that all was not well with the design and implementation of Demonetisation 2016.

Soon, there was a chorus of critical comments about the exercise from economists and commentators in India and abroad. Could a one-off demonetisation destroy the black economy or would it only attack the cash component of black money? Would not demonetisation and the cash scarcity that followed hurt the very people who could least afford to cope? (The meaning of black money, the importance of cash as a form of black money and the global experience with demonetisation are discussed in chapters 1–4.) In the barrage of commentary that followed, it was difficult to find many serious economists who approved of the measure. Indeed, even from within the government, there was silence from many economists.

As the economy was thrown out of gear, attention turned to the very rationale of the exercise. Was it the only way to attack black money? Were there other options to deal with counterfeit currency? Granted the need for secrecy, was there scope for doing it better?

As chapters 6 and 7 show, there were indeed options available for a far less disruptive exercise to achieve the stated objectives.

Shift in Narrative: Towards Digitalisation

The Prime Minister's speech of 8 November made no mention of electronic forms of monetary transactions (more commonly referred to as 'digitalisation'). The gazette notification on demonetisation also did not mention digitalisation. However, soon the narrative changed, and digitalisation became the *mantra* (see chapter 8).

The morning after the demonetisation announcement, on 9 November, many newspapers carried advertisements of mobile wallets on their front pages, welcoming the decision. The firms which operated in the digital sphere evidently knew a business opportunity when they saw one.

When the cash scarcity hit, with banks unable to provide cash even for the low allotments, the authorities displayed an insensitivity bordering on the callous. Within a few days, one advisory stated,

> Public are encouraged to switch over to alternative modes of payment, such as pre-paid cards, Rupay/Credit/Debit cards, mobile banking, internet banking. All those for whom banking accounts under Jan Dhan Yojana are opened and cards are issued are urged to put them to use. Such usage will alleviate the pressure on the physical currency and also enhance the experience of living in the digital world.

Digital transactions did indeed show a huge increase across platforms, especially among mobile wallets. But the GoI and Reserve Bank of India (RBI) should have been aware that access to digital platforms was very limited among people and that it was not going to change in a few days at a time when the public starved of cash were often struggling to make ends meet.

When the GoI found that it was losing control of the demonetisation narrative, it shifted to speaking about demonetisation ushering in a 'cash less' society, which, fortunately, later became a 'less cash' society. Soon the speeches of the Prime Minister and senior ministers shifted to the many benefits of moving away from cash towards using digital forms of payments.

A high-level committee of chief ministers was constituted to recommend ways to accelerate a shift to digitalisation. Charges on digital transactions up to a certain value were reduced. 'Lottery prizes' were announced to encourage use of credit/debit cards, mobile wallets, and the like. A bewildered public tried to adapt. Those who were comfortable with the digital platform expanded their use and those who could get access began to learn to use them. The larger population, however, struggled to manage with whatever little cash it could lay its hands on.

This shift to prioritising digitalisation over destruction of black money and the general confusion about why all this was being done allowed various conspiracy theories to be circulated about international forces and agencies driving the agenda. There was indeed a new global discussion on doing away with cash, but the context in the advanced countries was about dealing with criminal activities, which had little relevance to the digitalisation thrust in India after Demonetisation 2016. Finance would benefit from the charges it collected from digital transactions, but there is no evidence that it was behind the new digitalisation mantra.

There were two economic policy arguments advanced officially as well as independently linking digitalisation with demonetisation and setting forth a scenario of transformational change. One was that with digitalisation there would be greater 'formalisation' of the informal sector, transactions could be tracked, and therefore there would be greater tax receipts. The second argument was that with digitalisation, financial savings would enter the banking system and be available for an expansion in formal lending.

It would seem that the shift in the agenda towards digitalisation of transactions has now been cemented. Where the Union Budget for 2015–16 had a detailed listing of measures to be taken to tackle black money, the Union Budget for 2017–18 has another detailed listing of measures, this time for accelerating the pace of digitalisation.

An unusual aspect of the current digitalisation drive is that while RBI statistics showed that there was a boom in electronic transactions carried out by individuals in November and December 2016 (when cash was in short supply), these actually declined in January 2017. It appeared that once people who embraced digital transactions got hold of some cash, they gave up their newfound digital habits. The events of a single month do not make a trend, but this does indicate how much of a compulsion there was behind the digital spike of November and December 2016 and how much people were going to resist this compulsion.

THE SUFFERING

With 86 per cent of the currency in circulation made invalid and fresh currency initially available only in a trickle, it was inevitable that the hardship caused to people was immense. In the beginning, there was bewilderment over the suddenness and scale of the withdrawal of currency that was vital to their daily lives. The bewilderment was also about why they could not access their own savings in banks and why there were such tight controls on how much they could withdraw. It has also been speculated that a more long-lasting damage may have been to the faith that people had in currency, a faith shaken by the ease with which the government invalidated notes that were very much part of everyday use.

Demonetisation affected all sectors of the economy. The initial numbers on industrial production, area sowed for the winter rabi crop, tax collections and firm sales made for an unclear picture. By early 2017, it was clear that economic activity had been affected across the board. News began trickling in of adverse financial results of large and small firms in the organised sector. It was not only items of mass consumption that had taken a hit. Every single product and service seemed to have suffered a loss to a greater or lesser extent.[2]

The cash-dependent informal sector, which was home to 85 per cent of the workforce, was the most affected. The informal sector comprises agriculture, micro enterprises in rural India, micro enterprises in industry and services in urban India, and a

---

[2] The only exception was perhaps the firms offering mobile wallet services.

variety of low productivity activities in both rural and urban areas. It has self-employed family enterprises and small units working with a limited amount of hired labour. These were also the people who had only limited familiarity with and access to digital forms of payment.

The hardship of the people in the informal sector was felt in myriad ways, including in a loss of employment, and therefore of income and consumption. One impact that will come to light later is that the loss of employment as also delays in payment have led to a higher level of personal debt.

Government agencies were slow to measure the impact of demonetisation on the ground.[3] However, reporters from the media fanned out to different parts of the country, studied different economic sectors, and spoke with economic agents at all levels, with a special focus on people who were the most vulnerable to the shock. The media, under attack lately for trivialisation of issues, did itself proud with a rich documentation of the ground reality (for more, see chapter 9).[4]

The suffering of people could not be captured in estimates of the loss to gross domestic product (GDP). The full scale of the

---

[3] To the best of one's knowledge, the Planning Board of the Government of Kerala has been the only one (as of February 2017) to have undertaken a quick but detailed study of the impact of demonetisation on the local economy (Planning Board 2017).

[4] There was also a flowering of satire on social media. The frequent changes in the rules and regulations on Demonetisation 2016 and the extravagant claims at times of the GoI together offered material for much biting satire. There was unfortunately a good amount of fake news as well. There were hilarious ones like news of a chip being embedded in the new Rs 2,000 note which would allow authorities to track black money movement. There were more sinister ones like allegations that India had been surrounded by presses that had stored a massive amount of fake Indian currency notes, which would have undermined the economy if it were not for Demonetisation 2016.

disruptive impact of Demonetisation 2016 will be known only in the middle of 2017 when the first comprehensive estimates of GDP growth in fiscal (April–March) 2016–17 are released. The initial forecasts by government, private and multilateral agencies of the loss to GDP growth range from 0.25 to 0.50 per cent to as much as 2 to 3 per cent. However, since the informal sector is largely of low productivity, a major contraction in output would have a negligible impact on GDP growth but have a large impact on the work and incomes of those in this sector.

The big question was if this was a temporary disruption which, with the re-entry of cash, would take things back to normal. In early 2017, it was too early to come to definite conclusions. One fear was that many micro and small enterprises in the informal sector which operate on the margin could have been permanently damaged by the disruption.

The few by-elections held in November–December 2016 to Parliament, state assemblies, and local polls showed no clear negative impact on the fortunes of the ruling Bharatiya Janata Party (BJP). The big test was to come in the Assembly polls in Uttar Pradesh (UP), Punjab, Uttarakhand, Goa and Manipur in February–March 2017. The media reported simmering voter anger against Demonetisation 2016, but few were willing to extrapolate this anger onto an election outcome.

Interestingly, in December 2016, Demonetisation 2016 was the main subject of the Prime Minister's speeches in UP. But by February 2017, the subject had disappeared from his speeches as well as from those of the leading campaigners of the BJP.

POLITICS AND BLACK MONEY

The most unusual aspect of Demonetisation 2016 was that while people underwent hardship, they were unwilling to express their anger. Other than in isolated instances, there were no mass protests, as one would have expected following such a major economic shock administered by the GoI.

One explanation was that the narrative of Demonetisation 2016 had successfully been sold as action taken against the corrupt rich on behalf of the poor, and that this was a battle for the larger good. Indeed, the media reported that many of those badly affected bore their difficulties stoically, saying this was all for the good. Temporary hardship was acceptable since the evil of black money would now be vanquished.

Demonetisation 2016 caught all political parties by surprise. Immediately after the announcement, almost the entire opposition was ranged against the GoI, criticising it for what it saw as an ill-conceived decision.

It was soon apparent that this was a decision that had been taken in a small and closed circle. The Prime Minister, who took personal ownership of it, appeared to stake his reputation on demonetisation.

Criticism of Demonetisation 2016, loud as it was, did not seem to stick because the political opposition was unable to offer any argument that could not be dubbed as in favour of black money. With the Prime Minister successful in portraying Demonetisation 2016 as part of a battle between the poor and the corrupt rich, the Opposition position was all the more weakened. Though the Opposition tried to organise protests and there was even a one-day national bandh on 28 November 2016 to express anger against Demonetisation 2016, these were largely weak gestures.

There was no debate in Parliament in the Winter Session of 2016, which was held soon after the demonetisation decision. The Opposition saw a new vulnerability in the government, but criticism took the form of not letting Parliament function because the Prime Minister himself did not seem eager to engage with Parliament. The sorry outcome was that a 'non-debate' on Demonetisation 2016 (other than one critique by former Prime

Minister Manmohan Singh) led to a washout of the Winter Session and marked yet another low in the functioning of Parliament in India.

While the government and the Opposition clashed over the pros and cons of Demonetisation 2016, there was a strange silence in the debate though it is well known that a huge amount of black money is expended in elections.

Commentators in the media did highlight this aspect and argued that unless the use of unaccounted money in election campaigns was addressed, there was going to be limited success in destroying black money. There was another side to black money in politics that was absent even in media comment—the generation and use of black money when political personalities enter business or when business persons enter politics. Black money as a 'source' and 'sink' in electoral politics was something that no one in the polity seemed to want to address.[5] It was almost as if everyone had a stake in the prevailing system, which they did not wish to disturb. Chapter 10 steps into this territory to address this imbalance in the discourse.

Money Laundering and the Return of the Taxman

There was Rs 14.18 lakh crore (trillion) in denominations of Rs 500 and Rs 1,000 in circulation when they were demonetised on 8 November 2016. The government did not offer an estimate of how much of this currency it thought would not return to the banking system. Informal estimates were that the GoI expected 25 to 30 per cent of this Rs 14.18 lakh crore (trillion) to not

[5] I owe the idea of black money in politics functioning as both a source and sink to V. Bhaskar.

be surrendered, which would have made it the black money unearthed by the exercise.

In the event, a much larger amount than expected seemed to have been deposited in the banks and much sooner than expected. On 12 December, the RBI reported that as of 10 December 2016—less than five weeks after the announcement and three weeks before the deadline of 30 December—as much as Rs 12.44 lakh crore (Rs 12.44 trillion) or 88 per cent of the Rs 14.18 trillion had already been deposited in the banking system. When the final numbers are officially revealed, they may show that very little of black money held as cash was 'extinguished'.[6] One view was that even if more black money had not been exposed, it had now come into the formal financial sector and was therefore a development for the better.

People were perplexed that large amounts of cash had returned to the banking system with so much ease. It was evident that the rich and corrupt who had black money as cash had found ingenious as well as simple ways to deposit their illicit money in banks. Money laundering appeared to have taken place on a large scale. While ordinary people stood for hours in queues to exchange their high denomination notes for new currency notes, holders of black money in cash were able to beat the system. Figures revealed in Union Finance Minister Arun Jaitley's 2017–18 budget speech gave an idea of the scale of large cash deposits

---

[6] While estimates of the money returned to the banking system were regularly provided by the RBI between 8 November and 10 December, this stopped after 10 December. The GoI cast doubts on the validity of these estimates, arguing that there may be some double counting and the numbers needed to be checked. As of the second week of February 2017, there was still no official news of how much had returned to the banking system. Some news reports said that over 90–95 per cent of the value of the Rs 500 and Rs 1,000 currencies in circulation had been deposited in the banks.

made in banks between 8 November and 30 December 2016. About 1.09 crore bank accounts received cash deposits of between Rs 2 lakh and Rs 80 lakh (average of Rs 5.03 lakh). Higher up, 1.48 lakh accounts received deposits of more than Rs 80 lakh (average deposit size of Rs 3.31 crore). The larger deposits were going to be investigated for the source of funds.

Perhaps recognising the scale of money laundering that was going on, midway through the period scheduled for depositing cash in banks, the GoI came out with a new amnesty scheme for holders of black money, the Pradhan Mantri Garib Kalyan Yojana 2016 (PMGKY). The aim seemed to be to get those who had laundered their black money to take advantage of the amnesty and come clean. The success of this scheme will be known only when it ends on 31 March 2017.

The laundering of black money into the banking system raised fears that the tax authorities would be asked to deliver on what Demonetisation 2016 could not achieve. In the first two-three months after demonetisation there were periodic reports of raids across the country (including one on the residence of the Chief Secretary of the Government of Tamil Nadu) and seizures of black money in the form of cash and assets. While what was seized ran into crores, they were trifling sums compared to the magnitude of black money that the GoI had been seeking to extinguish.

In December 2016, the tax authorities created and publicised an email address which citizens could write to about individuals/organisations with black money. Within days, the Income Tax (IT) department had received thousands of emails. This appeared to take its reliance on information from the public to a new level, and there were fears that this would encourage inquiries on a false basis.

The large amount of information collected when deposits were made on an unprecedented scale after 8 November 2016 began to be analysed soon thereafter. After the Union Budget for 2016–17 was presented, a new drive, 'Operation Clean Money', was launched. In the first stage, holders of 18 lakh accounts were asked to explain within a week the source of funds for the deposits made between 8 November and 31 December 2016. It was clear that this was the first step to unearth black money laundered after Demonetisation 2016. But could an under-staffed IT department be able to analyse millions of bank accounts, the returns of the holders of these accounts and identify those with black money? Or would it give up and instead pick on randomly chosen accounts to show that it was doing something?

The big fear was whether the new drive would lead to new and higher levels of harassment. There were voices within the government as well cautioning against asking the IT department to go all out and unearth black money without putting any safeguards in place against harassment of the honest taxpayer. The anxiety was that the past record of the IT department in harassing taxpayers and at the same time being susceptible to pressures would rear a new ugly head to prove that Demonetisation 2016 was a success.

Indeed, soon after demonetisation was announced, talk that gold holdings would be targeted by the tax authorities led to a round of clarifications and explanations. (The place of gold in Indian society and the GoI's approach to the yellow metal are discussed in chapter 14.)

RBI, Cash, and Banks

Unlike in 1978 when the GoI issued an ordinance on demonetisation, in 2016 the RBI central board recommended the demonetisation of Rs 500 and Rs 1000 currency notes, which the government then acted on. Questions were asked if the RBI board had applied its mind to the issue or only did what the GoI wanted it to do. This marked the beginning of a period of intense public scrutiny of the functioning of the RBI.

Two issues engaged the public. The first was a matter of great importance—the availability of cash or rather the lack of availability of cash. Since printing and distribution of currency was the responsibility of the central bank, public concern inevitably turned to the RBI when for weeks on end there was not enough cash available in ATMs and banks. The mismatch between the currency printing capacity available and the scale of 'remonetisation' required, led to questions about the extent of prior planning that had been carried out. Chapter 11 has more on the issues of cash, money and liquidity.

The second issue was the frequency with which rules and regulations on currency exchange, and cash withdrawals were changed in the first eight weeks. Initially, it was the finance ministry officials who publicly announced changes in what was part of the RBI's domain, the changes being subsequently included in RBI notifications. These frequent changes not only inconvenienced people, they also reflected poorly on the central bank, which otherwise had a reputation for professionalism of a very high order.

The interface between the RBI/GoI and the public was the banks. It was the banking system that experienced the full brunt of Demonetisation 2016 from many directions. It had the responsibility of handling the exchange/deposit of a massive number of demonetised currency notes. It had to deal with a public that wanted to withdraw its savings in new currency notes, which were very much in short supply. It had to cope with public anger over the process taking too long. For many weeks, banks did nothing other than exchange/deposit/distribute currency notes. The staff of banks was under extreme strain and though there were occasional reports of them conniving in money laundering, they did what they were expected to do admirably (chapter 12).

A different and yet very important aspect relating to the balance sheet of the central bank surfaced in the first week after demonetisation.

The currency that the central bank issues is a liability. So, if a very large amount of the high denomination currency in circulation was not going to be surrendered, or be 'extinguished', would the corresponding reduction in central bank liability result in a gain to the government through a transfer from the asset side of the RBI's balance sheet? With the RBI initially silent, there was much speculation on whether the government would receive 'windfall gains'. Would the GoI distribute this across all Jan Dhan bank account holders? Would this then be a redistribution of resources from the public to the private sector, from the rich to the poor?

A lack of clarity on what constitutes the RBI balance sheet and where it stands in the larger macro-economic balance sheet allowed the discussion to go in different directions. Chapter 13 sheds light on what could follow from any reduction in the liabilities of the RBI following demonetisation.

Economic Survey on Demonetisation

The *Economic Survey* of 2016–17 contained the first government assessment of the impact of Demonetisation 2016. The *Survey* contained a separate chapter on the subject with a catchy title, 'Demonetisation: To Deify or Demonise?' It identified three issues in the public debate, but addressed only one—the short- and medium-term economic impact. And even within that, it steered clear of dealing with broader welfare dimensions.[7] The short-term

[7] The other two issues the *Survey* identified were those relating to design and implementation (the subject of chapter 7 here) and those dealing with the broader economic vision underpinning demonetisation. The non-economic impact, which too the *Survey* did not deal with, is discussed briefly in chapter 9.

economic impact was estimated to be a 0.25 to 0.50 per cent loss in GDP in 2016–17.

The *Survey* identified three long-term markers of success of Demonetisation 2016, none of which was part of the original objectives of reducing corruption and black money, and neutralising counterfeit currency. The first marker of success will be an increase in digital payment methods among individuals, the second a reduction in the cash-GDP ratio. The third and most important marker of success will be an increase in the number of income taxpayers and the amount of tax collected.

As pointed out earlier, digitalisation of payments emerged as an important part of the government's agenda midway through Demonetisation 2016, and has since come to be seen as the most important medium-term objective. The GoI highlighted this a few weeks after demonetisation was announced, the *Economic Survey* saw definite gains from digitalisation, and the finance minister made it a focus area of the Union Budget for 2017–18.[8]

On the whole, the *Survey* remained ambivalent about whether major gains would be realised from Demonetisation 2016. The gains seemed contingent on a number of complementary steps being taken. The document also skirted the issue of whether demonetisation should have been carried out or not. It made the unexceptional argument that the long-term benefits must be maximised while the short-term costs should be minimised.

The restrictions on cash withdrawals should be removed soon, the *Economic Survey* argued, and there must be no restrictions on the availability of cash (that is, the government should not use the opportunity to hold back the supply of cash). The benefits are seen as digitalisation of electronic payments (yet again).

---

[8] If there is one thing the *Survey* is unambiguously positive about in its discussion of Demonetisation 2016, it is what it sees as a rise in electronic payments among individuals who earlier did not access this platform.

If Demonetisation 2016 was a stick then, the *Survey* argued, it should be accompanied by carrots such as lower personal and corporate tax rates, lower stamp duties, and a tax administration that is more accountable and acts with less discretion.

In the end, there is no definite answer the *Survey* could offer to the question 'Deify or Demonise?'

Union Budget 2017–18

The public debate that followed immediately after the demonetisation of high denomination notes on 8 November 2016 asked if such a measure by itself would do much to destroy black money in India. It was pointed out at the time that Demonetisation 2016, first, dealt only with the black money held in the form of cash, and, second, it did nothing to stop the generation of black money.

Perhaps in response to such criticism, the Prime Minister and many union ministers stated that Demonetisation 2016 was going to be only the first of a series of measures that would address black money.

If the Union Budget was to be the GoI's platform to outline what was to follow, it had little to say on that. Compare the Union Budget for 2015–16 with the Union Budget for 2017–18 and we find that while the former had announced a package of measures on black money, there was barely a mention in the latter. One exception was the proposals on political party finance (more on this in the next section). Another was the changes proposed on taxation of long-term capital gains made through share transfers in unlisted companies, which was aimed at ending money laundering through manipulation of share prices in shell companies.

The focus, to emphasise again, had shifted entirely to digitalisation of payments. There was an outlining of a whole series of steps the GoI was going to carry out to take digitalisation forward. The Union Budget for 2017–18 seemed to only find it important to use digitalisation to increase tax collections and financial savings.

Meanwhile, black money seems to have disappeared from the agenda.

The Budget and Political Party Finance

All political parties were silent during the public debate on Demonetisation 2016 about politics and black money. The Union Budget for 2017–18 aimed to address this silence by addressing political party finance.

Chapter 10 discusses the two-way connection between politics and business, and how black money has come to play an important role in this arena. The rules so far facilitate anonymity in individual donations of up to Rs 20,000, which can be given in cash, and this is seen as a route for channelling black money to political parties.

The Union Budget for 2017–18 had two concrete proposals on party finance.

One is a reduction in the ceiling for individual cash donations to Rs 2,000, as earlier recommended by the Election Commission of India (ECI). The practice so far has been to split up large collections of black money into individual donations, each less than Rs 20,000 so that the anonymity of the source is maintained. The new rule only makes this more difficult; it does not prevent it. There is a need to encourage small donations, but there is no need to maintain anonymity however small the donation. The Rs 2,000 rule will continue to keep the door open for black money.

The second proposal in the budget is to issue 'electoral bonds'. It would seem that the idea is for the RBI to issue electoral bonds, which individuals/organisations can purchase at banks (by cheque, thus keeping out unaccounted cash). The buyers can donate these bonds to political parties, which can deposit them only into their bank accounts. Because they are bearer bonds, the banks will know the identity of the buyer, but the political parties receiving them would not know who the donor is. This opacity about the donor may free the political party from returning favours. However, the interests of transparency are not met by such features. In any case, which donor would not want his identity to be known to the recipient political party?

Indeed, the proposed opacity of the donor-recipient relationship has led commentators to point out that a strange situation is likely to develop. The donor's books will only record that bonds have been bought, they will not record who the bonds have been donated to. The political party receiving the bonds will record receipt of the bonds but the identity of the benefactor will not be known. This is a perfect cover of anonymity for pay-offs to take place. It would seem that the business-politics links are going to be strengthened and not weakened with such 'reform'.

***

By early 2017, India's society and economy had started limping back to a routine of sorts. Yet, the short- and long-term effects of 'notebandi' had not played themselves out fully. The saga of Demonetisation 2016 will continue to unfold in the months and years ahead.

Section I

— *one* —

Black Money and the Black Economy

We all seem to know that 'black money' is something illegal and holding it is unethical. But what exactly is it and how is it produced?

Black Money or Black Income

Black money is best understood as income that is earned through two different processes. One kind is where income is generated from illegal activities such as extortion, trafficking, drugs and corruption. Another kind is where it has been earned in legal activities, but on which taxes and other dues are not paid to the government authorities at the central, state or local levels.

Black money then is either income generated from illegal activities, or income generated from legal actvities which then becomes illegal because it is not reported to the tax authorities.[1]

The relative importance of each kind of black money varies from one society to another, depending on the extent to which

[1] This is more or less the same definition as that contained in the fine 2012 White Paper on Black Money, prepared by the Ministry of Finance. Black money there is defined as that which 'is not fully legitimate in the hands of the owner...for two possible reasons' (p. 1). One reason is that the black money may have been generated from illegitimate activities like 'crime, drug trade, terrorism and corruption'. The second reason is that it may have been generated by 'failing to pay the dues to the exchequer in one form or the other'.

criminal activities are present and the degree to which taxes are evaded.

In India, both sets of activities are prevalent to a large extent. Illegitimate activities in the form of corruption among government and elected officials are widely prevalent. So too is tax evasion at the central and state levels, and also in the payment of direct and indirect taxes. It is not easy to estimate the relative size of the two streams of black money, or income, nor has apparently anyone attempted to do so.

In common parlance, both the income that is earned and the wealth that is accumulated from this income are referred to as black money.

The illegal or unaccounted income that is accumulated over time is held as wealth in different kinds of assets—real estate that is land, etc., gold, jewellery, *benami*[2] bank deposits, bank accounts hidden from the tax authorities, or plain cash. This too is called black money.

These assets can be held at home or abroad, with the holder of black wealth taking a decision based both on where it is best hidden and/or where it can be put to better use.

Strictly speaking, since one is income earned and the other an asset, the term black money should not be used to refer to both. But since black money is commonly used to refer to both income and wealth, this book too uses the term 'black money' interchangeably, and wherever necessary makes it clear if it is the illegal income or wealth that is being discussed.[3]

---

[2] The word *benami* literally means 'without a name'. In tax-related usage, it means that an asset may be purchased by one person, but it is held in the name of another (real or fictitious). This is done to hide the real ownership of the asset.

[3] The 2012 White Paper also clubs both income and wealth under the term 'black money': 'For the purpose of this document, "black money" can be defined as assets or resources that have neither been reported to

THE BLACK ECONOMY

There is black money and there is the 'black economy'[4]. This part of the economy comprises the set of activities which generate black money or the activities into which the legal-turned-illegal money flows. The black economy is also where the black money is employed in its illegal activities.

Black money generated in trafficking, for instance, may be ploughed back to expand operations, or could be invested in other illegal activities like smuggling, or used to bribe public officials to look away from the crimes being perpetrated.

Black money comes from the black economy, so if black money is to be removed from the economy, it is the black economy which must be destroyed, or conditions will have to be created such that it cannot survive. In other words, one-off attempts to flush out black money without regard to the underlying black economy will, even if successful, not prevent fresh generation of black money.

INTERCHANGEABILITY OF THE BLACK AND THE WHITE

There is a constant flow of money between white and black streams (Reddy 2016).

To give an example, a real estate developer, who is paid partly in cash for his sales and does not report this income to the tax authorities, may use these unaccounted funds in a variety of ways. S/he may use one part to pay a seller of cement in cash, who too

---

the public authorities at the time of their generation nor disclosed at any point of time during their possession' (p. 2).

[4] Internationally, the black economy is also variously referred to as the 'underground economy', the 'shadow economy', or simply as the 'illegal economy'. As we shall discuss briefly in chapter 3, in global discussions these terms have a slightly different meaning than in India.

wishes to hide this sale from the tax authorities. This part of the black money then circulates in the black economy. The cement, along with other legally paid for materials, may be used to build a group of flats for which all necessarily permissions have been obtained. Here, the black money is converted into an asset that is part of the 'white' or the legal economy.

A second part of the real estate developer's black money may be used to buy gold which is not reported and the last part kept in cash. So, these second and third parts of the black money of the real estate developer remain part of the black economy as unaccounted assets.

In the meanwhile, the trader of cement may use his cash income to pay his workers cash wages that are not reported in his books of account. The workers may use their wages to visit a store, buy groceries, demand and receive a receipt on which tax is shown as paid. Here, the black money of the trader gets converted, via certain purchases of the workers, into white money.

There is then both a constant back and forth movement of money in both forms, and therefore an intermingling of the legal and illegal activities. This interaction between and consequent conversion from one to the other, of black and white money could pose their own challenges to attempts to stamp out the black economy.

Black money in its asset form also moves back and forth across national borders. Black money generated at home can be taken out of the country and deployed abroad in some asset, or even kept as bank deposits. After a while it could be brought back to India through a 'legal' route like an offshore financial centre and invested as legal money in the domestic economy. This is called the 'round-tripping' of black money.

In an asset the illegal can also be embedded along with the legal. To return to our example of the real estate developer, when s/he sells a flat to a buyer, the price of the flat may cover both the legal expenditure as well as the expenditure incurred illegally such as payment made with black money for some of the cement. (The books of account may, however, tell a fake story.) Here then the black money used in construction is 'embedded' in the price of the flat. The buyer of the flat may pay for it from tax-paid income and by cheque and may possess in full a legal asset, but what s/he has paid for comes with an element of black money used in its construction that s/he may not be aware of.

When s/he sells the flat, s/he may be compelled by the buyer to accept a part of the payment in cash that has not been reported to the tax authorities. So here, through the various stages of production and sale, we have a combination of black and white (construction) money turning into white (first sale) money, and then again into black and white (second sale) money, a constant intermingling and moving back and forth of the money.

In various transactions, the 'stock' of black money contained in an asset on sale can be converted into a 'flow'. While stocks of black money, embedded or otherwise, can be held in different forms, the flows are often in cash. These were earlier entirely through cash. While conversions through cash flows continue to be important, new forms are now used. Increasingly, large value conversions of stocks into flows also take place through the financial system through sophisticated manipulation of accounts, and not through cash.

(In the textbooks, 'stocks' are assets and 'flows' are incomes. Here in the discussion of black money, we use flows in a different sense to convey the conversion into cash and also an intermingling of white and black.)

Forms of Generation of Black Money

The 2012 White Paper has a useful listing of the many ways in which black money is generated.

One is what it calls the 'crude' way in which income generated from illegal activities is hidden from the law. At a subsequent stage, this black money may be laundered using sophisticated methods, but in the first round it is just hidden from the law.

Another is what is called a more sophisticated approach in generating income from legal activities that is not reported to the tax authorities subsequently. This is done under the broad rubric of 'manipulation of accounts'.

The ways in which black money is generated have been acquiring an increasing sophistication, especially in financial practices that cross national borders. They include transfer pricing in trade, money laundering through trade, use of tax havens/ offshore financial centres and investment through derivative instruments like participatory notes (PNs).[5]

Extracts of the informative discussion on the various sophisticated ways in which black money is generated and hidden from detection at home and abroad are presented in Annexure IV of this book.

The White Paper also identifies some sectors as more 'vulnerable' to the generation of black money. These include: (i) land and real estate transactions, (ii) bullion and jewellery transactions, (iii) financial market transactions, (iv) public

[5] Participatory notes, or PNs as they are called, are instruments issued by Foreign Institutional Investors (FIIs) to inividual investors abroad. The FIIs invest in the Indian market and the value of the PNs reflects the value of the underlying investments. The PNs allow the investors to hold investments in Indian equities anonymously. Indian regulators, therefore, do not know who the ultimate owners of the PNs are. It is believed that much of the investment in PNs is really round-tripping of money illegally held abroad by Indians (a more detailed definition is in Annexure IV; the Annexure also describes and explains the other types of financial transactions like transfer pricing, which are now used to generate black money).

procurement, (v) the non-profit sector and (vi) the informal sector with its cash economy. It would be useful to note here that the informal sector is only one of the many sectors vulnerable to the generation of black money.

The relative importance of these sectors for the generation of black money has changed over the years. Earlier, bullion (gold) trade was an important source of generation of black money. In the recent years, real estate, financial market transactions, corruption in public procurement (civil contracts, defence imports) and practices in the non-profit sector (education institutes and hospitals run by trusts) have become more important for black money generation.

— two —

Size of the Black Economy in India

It is in the nature of what is sought to be measured that there is no agreement on how to measure the black economy and that there is also no definite estimate of the size of the black economy in India.

Academics, research institutions and government-appointed committees have all sought to measure India's black economy since the mid-1950s. The numbers vary a lot, depending on both the definition used and the methodology followed for its estimation.

The White Paper has the most comprehensive summary of the different estimates made in India (GoI 2012: 9–16). It would be useful to present here some of the details of the summary along with some more recent estimates.

Measuring the Black Economy

There are four broad methods to measure black economy (ibid.: 9–10). They are:

(i) The input-output method (which uses norms on how much of inputs are used to produce a unit of output) is adopted to estimate what the size of the economy should be. This is compared with the size of the economy as measured in the official National Accounting System (NAS). The difference is taken to be the size of the black economy in a particular year.

(ii) The monetarist approach in which the gross domestic product (GDP) estimate of the NAS is compared to that worked out based on the money supply and the velocity of money (the number of times a currency is used for transactions in a year). The difference between the two is another figure on the black economy.

(iii) The survey approach in which consumption in a sample is measured and the total consumption estimated. The difference between this figure and the official NAS estimate of consumption is the quantum of the black economy.

(iv) The fiscal approach in which the size of the black economy in each sector is estimated and then totalled for the entire economy.

Each of these approaches calls for assumptions of many kinds; so what one ends up with are very different numbers.

ESTIMATES OF THE BLACK ECONOMY

The White Paper also presents estimates of the size of India's black economy (ibid.: 10–13).

The first attempt at measuring India's black economy was undertaken by the British economist Nicholas Kaldor in 1956. In post-Independence India, the first official estimate of black money was made by the Wanchoo Direct Taxes Enquiry Committee in 1971. The committee estimated the income on which tax was evaded at Rs 700 crore in 1961–62 and Rs 1,000 crore in 1965–66. (It also made projections for 1968–69.) This works out to be 3.7 per cent and 3.4 per cent of GDP in the two years, respectively.

Subsequently, there were many other estimates. D. K. Rangnekar, a member of the Wanchoo Committee, gave his dissenting estimate which was 40–50 per cent higher, and later another economist O. P. Chopra prepared estimates for a period of 17 years, between 1960–61 and 1976–77. The latter saw an increase in the quantum of unaccounted income from 6.5 per cent of the gross national product (GNP) to 11.4 per cent of GNP in 1960–61 and 1976–77 respectively (see Table 2.2 of the White Paper for a comparison of the different estimates.)

Subsequently, in 1985, the National Institute of Public Finance and Policy (NIPFP), on behalf of the Ministry of Finance, prepared the most well-known estimates for black economy. These estimates prepared by a group headed by the economist Shankar Acharya estimated the black economy to be larger: 15–18 per cent of GDP in 1975–76, 18–21 per cent in 1980–81 and 19–21 per cent in 1983–84. The estimates also excluded illegal income generated from criminal activities like smuggling, extortion, corruption—these are activities that strictly speaking should also be covered in any estimate of the black economy.

The government commissioned three studies from three independent organisations for the preparation of the 2012 White Paper. The results of those studies have not been made public, though media reports of the estimates of one of the studies placed the black income in 2014 at as high as 75 per cent of sectoral GDP (*The Hindu* 2014).

Some recent independent estimates put the numbers even higher. Economist Arun Kumar, using the fiscal approach, has attempted to put together a series from 1980 to 2012, in which the relative size of the black economy in India, he shows, rises from 21 per cent of GDP in 1980, to as much as 62 per cent of GDP in 2012.

With such widely varying numbers, it seems that the only agreement across various studies is that the size of the black economy in India is large and has been growing over the decades.

There have also been estimates prepared internationally of the size of the black economy in India. As will be discussed in the next chapter, these estimates are based on a certain conception and measurement of what is called the shadow economy. They do not cover what is called 'pure tax evasion' as also criminal activities and are, therefore, of limited purpose for assessing the size of the black economy in India, though the White Paper refers to them.

If measurement of the domestic black economy is difficult, that of illicit outflows is even more complex. The estimates have been of a total outflow of $88 billion between 1971 and 1997 ($5.5 billion a year), and another of an even higher figure of $22 billion per year between 2002 and 2006. But according to a critical discussion in the 2012 White Paper, such estimates appear to be made on very many assumptions, some of which may be very unrealistic (GoI 2012: 14–16). Hence, they may not be useful even as orders of magnitude.

— three —

Size of the Shadow Economy in the World

Black money is not unique to India. It is found in different forms and sizes across the world. Governments world over grapple to minimise it.

It goes under different names across the world—the 'shadow economy', or 'underground economy' or 'parallel economy' or even the 'grey economy'. These also have a slightly different meaning than black money or the black economy as it is referred to in India. In the advanced countries, the shadow economy—the most commonly used term—refers to the informal economy rather than to the larger set of illegal activities which in India include corruption and tax evasion in the formal sector.

Globally, efforts to understand the black economy have had to face the same problems as in India. How do you measure it when it is in the nature of the beast that it is hidden from the law? Thus, for one recent study with a focus on corruption, crime and organised fraud,

> There are two different definitions of the informal economy, the economic definition, which defines the informal sector as a sector that does not contribute to the national tax revenue and the economy; and the legal definition, which defines the black or forbidden economy (penalized by the law). (Edlebacher, Kratcoski and Dobovšek 2016: 1)

Neither definition of the informal sector would apply to India, where a larger part of this sector is driven more by survival than by criminal activities or tax evasion.

INTERNATIONAL ESTIMATES OF THE SHADOW ECONOMY

The focus on the informal sector as understood in the advanced countries means that a restrictive definition is used in the study of the shadow economy.

For a study of the shadow economy across the world,

> ... we follow recent studies that adopt a narrower definition of the underground economy, "which includes all market-based legal production of goods and service that are deliberately concealed from public authorities to avoid the payment of income, value added or other taxes, to avoid payment of social security contributions, having to meet certain legal labor market standards, such as minimum wages, maximum working hours, and safety standards, and complying with certain administrative procedures". (Singh, Jain-Chandra Mohommad 2012, citing Schneider, Buehn and Montenegro 2010)

Therefore, many of the international studies that try to understand the shadow economy look more closely at informal activities which do not pay tax in countries where the tax threshold is low. This is unlike in the developing countries—including in low middle income and large countries like India—where the threshold for both direct and indirect tax payments can be fairly high.

The studies of the shadow economy tend to exclude study of income from criminal activities and/or the extent of what is called 'pure tax evasion' from financial transactions.

A 2012 international survey on the shadow economy has very clear exclusion criteria,

> Pure tax evasion via financial transactions is excluded from our analysis as it does not render added value—and is usually not meant—when someone is talking about the shadow economy. (Schneider and Enste 2013: 10)

Pure tax evasion in India would form a significant part of income creation in the black economy.

This approach to exclude pure tax evasion from measurement seems to be derived from a landmark 1997 study of the shadow economy in Canada which made this distinction,

> Pure tax evasion (PTE) involves non-reporting, understatement, or misreporting of taxable income, profits, or sales, but unlike UGE (underground economic) activity, PTE involves no labour input or no change of mode of business operation relative to the legitimate economy. Some PTE activity is related to extreme financial manipulation that goes beyond the bounds of legal tax avoidance. Other PTE occurs in conventional, legitimate businesses that underreport their receipts or overstate their expenses. Still other PTE stems from misreporting such events as intrafamilial transfers for tax purposes or misrepresenting the type, source, or timing of receipts. (Lippert and Walker 1997: 296)

Tax evasion of the kind described above is dealt with by authorities in the advanced countries separately from that involving tax evasion arising from activities in the shadow economy. This is different in India, where both kinds of tax evasion would lead to the creation of black money and are of concern to the same tax and law-enforcement authorities.

Hence, international country-wise estimates of the shadow economy which cover India as well must be treated with some caution.

One World Bank Working Paper that has been cited widely in recent years adopts precisely such a restricted definition,

> ... the shadow economy includes all market-based legal production of goods and services that are deliberately concealed from public authorities for any of the following reasons:
> (1) to avoid payment of income, value added or other taxes,
> (2) to avoid payment of social security contributions,
> (3) to avoid having to meet certain legal labor market standards, such as minimum wages, maximum working hours, safety standards, etc., and
> (4) to avoid complying with certain administrative procedures, such as completing statistical questionnaires or other administrative forms.
>
> This paper utilizes a more precise definition of the shadow economy so as not to deal with typical underground, classical economic crime activities, which are all illegal actions that fit the characteristics of crimes like burglary, robbery, drug dealing, etc. Also, this paper does not focus on tax evasion or tax compliance due to time and length constraints, and the fact that tax evasion is a subject on which a lot of research has already been undertaken. (Schneider, Buehn and Montenegro 2010: 2)

This study of the shadow economy in 162 countries between 1999 and 2007 puts its size in India at an average of 22.4 per cent of GDP (1999–2006) compared to the global average of between 32 and 34 per cent.

The shadow economy as understood in the advanced countries is, therefore, not the same as the black economy in India which covers a wider universe. The informal sector which appears to constitute the shadow economy in the advanced countries is also a different one in India and other developing countries. Its organisation, motivation and place in the Indian economy are very different from that in the advanced countries where it is seen solely as a set of activities operating beyond the pale of the law in order to avoid payment of tax.

The World Bank Working Paper notes this in a limited manner,

> Large shadow economies in some developing countries are only to some extent an issue of tax burden and regulation, given the simple fact that the limited local economy means that citizens are often unable to earn a living wage in a legitimate manner. Working in the shadow economy is often the only way of achieving a minimal standard of living. (Schneider, Buehn and Montenegro 2010: 22)

THE MAGNITUDE OF GLOBAL CORRUPTION

Corruption is known in the developing countries to make a major contribution to the generation of black money. It is a global phenomenon affecting every country, even if its spread and depth varies. It is not easy to measure the incidence of corruption, which is why we do not have many magnitudes of the country-wise burden of corruption.

Transparency International, a non-government organisation (NGO), has been putting together the Corruption Perception Index (CPI). As its name implies, this is a measure of perceptions drawn from select organisations and individuals, and it does not measure the magnitude of corruption in each country. The CPI for 2015 is on expected lines with some of the poorest countries figuring the highest in the ranking (that is, very corrupt) and the countries drawn from the advanced countries figuring lower down (that is, very clean). India figures high in the rankings, occupying the 78th position among 168 countries. According to the 2015 edition of the Transparency International report, two out of three countries in the world suffer from a major corruption problem and these countries are home to more than 6 billion people.

There is even less of an understanding of how corruption is tied up with the shadow economy across the world. Some academic research says that in the advance countries, corruption and the shadow economy are substitutes, that is, demands for bribes drive activities underground. In the developing countries, the relationship is supposed to be complementary with the two feeding off each other.

We do not quite know how corruption and the shadow economy are connected across the world, but we do have country studies which look at corruption, the shadow economy and growth in individual countries.

One World Bank study looking at the experiences of Malawi (a low-income country) and Namibia (a middle-income country) in the context of 'ill-gotten money and the economy' shows how crime and tax evasion are hurting economic development. Among its conclusions are: 'T[t]ax evasion has an estimated magnitude of 8 to 12 per cent of GDP in Malawi and 9 per cent of GDP in Namibia. Corruption in Malawi is estimated to involve over 5 per cent of GDP. In Namibia, corruption is also significant, but we were not able to make a reliable estimate of the macroeconomic magnitude. However, several suspected (multi)million dollar corruption cases have been discovered in recent years' (p. 82). It goes on to add: 'Using AML [anti-money laundering] as an additional tool to fight corruption and tax evasion is likely to have a direct effect on recovering stolen money or lost revenue. Experience has proved this to be true in both Malawi and Namibia, but also globally' (p. 82).

— *four* —

Indian and Global Experiences with Demonetisation

The use of the term 'demonetisation' can be traced back to the mid-nineteenth century. It is derived from French and Latin 'from *dé-* (expressing reversal) + Latin *moneta* "money"' (Oxford Dictionaries Online).

Its dictionary meaning is to 'deprive (a coin or precious metal) of its status as money' (ibid.). The most common usage now is to describe an action under which a currency is deprived of its legal status as money.[1]

One type of such demonetisation takes place when the value of a currency has been debased by high inflation. The old currency is then replaced by a new one altogether. A fairly recent example is the replacement in Brazil in 1994 of the Cruzeiro Real by the New Real, in the drive to combat high inflation.

A variant of this kind of demonetisation is when the old currency is replaced by a new one that has been adopted as part of a monetary union of a number of countries. The most well-known example is the adoption of the Euro after the individual currencies of the members of the European Monetary Union (EMU) were demonetised.

---

[1] It is also used in some contexts to refer to a return to a barter economy; the term has been used to describe conditions in Russia during the mid-1990s when a loss of faith in the Russian rouble led to consumers adopting the barter system.

The second type of demonetisation is about swapping one or more currency denominations for another provided the holder can demonstrate the legality of her stock of the older notes. Such swaps can be accompanied by the introduction of a new series of currency notes of different denominations—lower, higher or of the same value. Since this is not 'demonetisation' in the historical sense of the term, the exchange is also referred to as 'delegalisation' of the older tender accompanied by an exchange of equal value, a 'currency swap'.

In the first type of demonetisation, all denominations are delegalised and the exchange rate of the new for the old is set by the central bank. In the second type, some or all denominations are delegalised and the exchange is of equal value.

In this book, the term demonetisation is used in its contemporary and commonly accepted form whereby currencies of certain denominations are no longer legal tender, but holders of the old currency can exchange them at the central bank for either newer currencies or for new series of the old currencies. To anticipate the discussion of the three episodes of demonetisation that India has experienced since 1946, in all the three instances demonetisation has been of this kind. Certain currencies—in all cases of a higher demonetisation—have been rendered devoid of legal tender; holders of the older higher denomination notes have had to exchange them for currency notes of a lower denomination or for new series/denominations.

The most striking periods of demonetisation have taken place when a currency has lost value and faith as during periods of very high inflation—the experience in Germany during the 1920s being the most well-known, when the old currency was replaced by a new one.

In the past 20–30 years, countries which have demonetised their currencies have included the Soviet Union/Russia, Brazil, Ghana, Nigeria, Zimbabwe and Myanmar. All of them have happened during periods of financial crises arising from a loss of faith in the currency. Thus, in Zimbabwe, for instance, in June 2015, much after the introduction of the multiple currency system or 'dollarization', the Reserve Bank of Zimbabwe demonetised the Zimbabwean dollar (Reserve Bank of Zimbabwe 2015).

Soon after India demonetised its high denomination currencies in early November 2016, Venezuela too demonetised its high value 100 Bolivar, and currency holders had to exchange their notes for a new currency. However, following widespread protests, a notice period of three days for exchange was lifted and demonetisation was postponed (at the time of writing) to January 2017.

The Indian experience has been quite different. The three cases of demonetisation that have taken place have had nothing to do with hyperinflation and loss of faith in the rupee.[2]

1946 Demonetisation

In 1946, the GoI, following the withdrawal of the 10 pound note in England after the end of the Second World War, decided to demonetise high denomination notes in India as a strategy to combat tax evasion. On 12 January, an ordinance was issued demonetising currency notes of Rs 500, Rs 1,000 and Rs 10,000 denominations. The holders of these notes were given time first until mid-February and then until mid-April to exchange their high denomination notes at the RBI.

However, the drive to extinguish the holdings of illegally accumulated cash was not successful. According to the official

---

[2]The presentation here of the 1946 and 1978 experiences, unless otherwise indicated, is drawn largely from the official RBI histories of the period. For 1946, see section 'Currency and Coinage Matters' in Chapter 21 titled 'Monetary Management and Allied Issues' in volume 1. For 1978, Section 'Demonetisation of High Denomination Notes' in Chapter 9 titled 'Currency Notes' in volume 3.

history, in the end, less than 10 per cent of the value of the high denomination notes was not presented to the RBI,

> It was really not a revolutionary measure and even its purpose as a minatory and punitive gesture towards black-marketing was not effectively served. There was no fool-proof administrative method by which a particular note brought by an individual could be proved as the life-savings of the hard-working man who presented it or established as the sordid gains of a black-marketeer. Another loophole of which considerable advantage was taken was the exemption of the Princely States from scrutiny or questioning when such notes were presented by them. In the end, out of a total issue of Rs 143.97 crores, notes of the value of Rs 134.9 crores were exchanged up to the end of 1947 as mentioned in the Report of the Board of Directors of the Reserve Bank. Thus, notes worth only Rs 9.07 crores were probably "demonetised", not having been presented. It was more of "conversion", at varying rates of profits and losses than "demonetisation". (RBI 1970: 708–09)

1978 DEMONETISATION

The next experience was in 1978, when the government resorted to demonetisation of Rs 1,000, Rs 5,000 and Rs 10,000 notes on 16 January. The decision was taken to flush out illegally accumulated holdings of cash, and took place within a year of a change in government in New Delhi; the RBI, however, was again not in favour of the demonetisation.

I. G. Patel, the RBI Governor back then, was apparently not in favour of this exercise. His view on this is documented in his book, *Glimpses of Indian Economic Policy: An Insider's View*, where he writes that he informed the then Finance Minister H. M. Patel that,

> ... such an exercise seldom produces striking results. Most people who accept illegal gratification or are otherwise the recipients of black money do not keep their ill-gotten earnings in the form of

> currency for long. The idea that black money or wealth is held in the form of notes tucked away in suitcases or pillow cases is naïve. And in any case, even those who are caught napping—or waiting—will have the chance to convert the notes through paid agents as some provision has to be made to convert at par notes tendered in small amounts for which explanations cannot be reasonably sought. But the gesture had to be made, and produced much work and little gain. (p. 159 cited in RBI 2005: 451)

More recently, in the context of the 8 November 2016 demonetisation, the after-effects of the 1978 episode have been subject to some analysis. For instance, one analysis by Nomura pointed out (citing other research) that of the high denomination notes demonetised at the time (constituting only 1.78 per cent of the total value of notes in circulation), only 14 per cent of them were not returned to the central bank.

The Nomura analysis also points out that banking and monetary trends after the event showed 'clear trends'.

Bank deposits rose sharply with a year-on-year (y-o-y) growth moving from 21.4 per cent y-o-y in December 1977 to 26.4 per cent by March 1978. This was followed by higher investment by the banks in government securities. This in turn 'pushed down the credit-deposit ratio from 69.6 per cent to 67.3 per cent'. Also, bank credit growth, though initially subdued, picked up within the next four months. That was not all. 'The drop in currency in circulation led to a moderation in reserve money growth (21.1 per cent to 11.7 per cent). Broad money supply (M3) did moderate, but not by much and, in fact, rose thereafter, in line with the credit surge. Finally, the adjustment in most of these parameters (deposit, investments and reserve money) was a one-time adjustment and they returned to their pre-demonetisation trends by mid-1978. Overall, we believe that the 1978 experience does throw some light on the possible trends we can expect in this exercise' (Varma 2016: 3–4).

Section II

— *five* —

Action on Black Money

Black money has always been in public consciousness in India. It has been more prominent since 2009 when the Supreme Court admitted a writ petition seeking directions to bring back funds that had been taken out of the country between 2002 and 2006. The Supreme Court hearings, official and unofficial reports about the illegal foreign bank deposits abroad, the occasional whistle-blowers' revelations about bank accounts in tax havens and the GoI's inaction, all together ensured that the issue of black money stayed in the public eye. It also became a part of political contention with the Opposition claiming that the government was not doing enough to curb black money.

The focus of public attention initially was on money illegally taken out of the country and kept in banks abroad or invested in assets in foreign countries. The writ petition in the Supreme Court too was about bank deposits illegally maintained by Indians abroad.

Following the hearings on the writ petition, which dealt with a couple of high-profile cases of alleged illegal holding of deposits in foreign banks, the Supreme Court in its first orders in July 2011 saw a 'lack of seriousness' on the part of the government in carrying out the necessary investigations. It also saw 'the absence of any satisfactory explanation of the slowness of the pace of investigation [by the Government of India], and lack of any credible answers as to why the respondents did not act with respect to those actions that were feasible' to bring back the funds maintained abroad. On those grounds, the Court, over the opposition of the government, converted a government-appointed high level committee to a Court-constituted Special Investigation Team (SIT) that would make a larger investigation into funds illegally kept abroad. The Supreme Court saw 'the need for continued, effective and day to day monitoring by an SIT constituted by this Court, and acting on behalf, behest and direction of this Court'.

The issue of black money was also repeatedly raised in Parliament, which persuaded the then government of Dr. Manmohan Singh to present the 2012 White Paper on Black Money, which has already been referred to in Section I of this book.

Recognising the importance the electorate was giving to the subject of black money, both the leading parties had agendas on black money in their manifestos for the 2014 Lok Sabha elections.

The Bharatiya Janata Party (BJP) said that its government, by reducing corruption, would minimise the generation of black money. The party focussed on wealth held abroad and promised, 'The process of bringing back black money to India what belongs to India, will be put in motion on priority'. The Congress Party manifesto mentioned, 'Serious and systematic efforts have been made by the Congress-led UPA government [2004 onwards] to track down and recover black money. This determined effort will continue unabated. We will appoint a Special Envoy to pursue this agenda'.

Measures to Recover Black Money

In the first full budget (2015–16) of the Narendra Modi government, Finance Minister Arun Jaitley in the budget speech highlighted measures to curb black money as an important part of his tax proposals. Jaitley outlined a number of steps to be undertaken, of which three were legislative proposals. These were proposals for a new law to punish concealment of income and assets held abroad, and for tightening the Prevention of Money Laundering Act, 2002 and the Benami Property Transactions Act, 1988. These were subsequently followed up on, and the legislative proposals were introduced in and approved by Parliament.

The subject did not receive the same attention in the Finance Minister's speech on Budget for 2016–17, though it did announce a new voluntary compliance scheme. The Narendra Modi government has in general sought to signal that it is serious about dealing with black money held abroad and at home, and about preventing further generation of black incomes.

In the meantime, the Supreme Court-directed SIT became operational in 2015. As of today, the Court continues to monitor the work of the SIT with regular hearings seeking responses from the government on information of accounts held illegally abroad, and to the revelations of the whistle-blowers.

The government has also been keeping Parliament informed of the legislative and administrative measures it has taken and proposes to take on the black economy.[1]

The steps have been in the form of re-negotiating international agreements, joining international conventions to fight black economy, and strengthening administrative action to deal with both illegal income generation and holding of such wealth within the country and abroad and, of course, enacting new legislation/amending existing legislation.

Briefly,

(i) The Black Money (Undisclosed Foreign Income and Assets) and Imposition of Tax Act was enacted in 2015 to penalise the concealment of foreign income. It also offered

[1] See, for instance, a detailed listing in the Answer to Unstarred Question 4528 in Lok Sabha, 12 August 2016.

a one-time settlement for disclosures of foreign income and assets.

(ii) The Prevention of Money-Laundering Act, 2002, was amended in 2015 through the Finance Act of the year to, among other things, enable 'attachment and confiscation of property equivalent in value held within the country where the property/proceeds of crime is taken or held outside the country'.

(iii) In May 2016, a protocol was signed to amend the Double Taxation Avoidance Agreement (DTAA) between India and Mauritius which, while protecting the investments made before April 2017 from capital gains taxation in India, would 'tackle the long pending issues of treaty abuse and round-tripping of funds attributed to the India-Mauritius treaty, curb revenue loss, prevent double non-taxation, streamline the flow of investment and stimulate the flow of exchange of information between India and Mauritius'. Subsequent to demonetisation, the government has signed similar protocols to modify existing DTAAs with Cyprus (November 2016) and Singapore (December 2016). All three are meant to deal with round-tripping of funds which had earlier been taken abroad illegally.

(iv) In October 2016, the Benami Property Transactions Act, 1988, was amended. The newly named Prohibition of Benami Property Transactions Act (PBPT), 1988, defines 'benami transactions, prohibits them and further provides that violation of the PBPT Act is punishable with imprisonment and fine'. The amended law 'prohibits recovery of the property held benami from benamidar by the real owner. (and) Properties held benami are liable for confiscation by the Government without payment of compensation'. The penalties for benami transactions have been increased in terms of both imprisonment and fines, and there is now a penalty for providing false information as well.

(v) In the Union Budget for 2016–17, a new amnesty/disclosure scheme was announced, and subsequently the 2016 Income Declaration Scheme (IDS) was operationalised to provide amnesty to tax evaders who maintained their illegal income/wealth within the country.

(vi) In response to media reports such as the 'Panama Papers' about the maintenance of assets held illegally abroad, the government set up a multi-agency task force to follow up on the disclosures.

Disclosures under Amnesty Schemes

The actual outcome of some of these measures has, however, been less than satisfying. For instance, the amnesty schemes of the Black Money (Undisclosed Foreign Income and Assets) and Imposition of Tax Act, 2015, and the Income Declaration Scheme of 2016 have had limited success when measured in terms of disclosures made.

An amount of Rs 4,164 crore of illegal income/wealth/income held abroad was declared under the temporary amnesty provisions of the 2015 Act. And an amount of Rs 65,250 crore has been provisionally declared (December 2016) under the 2016 Income Declaration Scheme.[2]

These schemes continued in the tradition of a long list of measures to provide amnesty. Past amnesty schemes include: (i) the National Housing Bank (Voluntary Deposits) Scheme, 1991, (ii) the Remittances in Foreign Exchange (Immunities) Scheme, 1991, and the India Development Bonds Scheme, 1991 and (iii)

[2] The Prime Minister's speech on 8 November announcing demonetisation mentioned a figure of Rs 125,000 crore as being disclosed under various measures.

the Voluntary Disclosure of Income Scheme (VDIS), 1997. There was a specific context for each of these schemes. The first was intended to mop up domestic black money in the midst of the fiscal/balance of payments crisis of 1991. The two schemes in the second category were aimed at mobilising foreign exchange resources during the balance of payment (BoP) crisis of 1991. The third was introduced in year when income tax rates were slashed for individuals and companies. The sums disclosed under those three sets of schemes were Rs 154 crore, Rs 6,400 crore (foreign exchange equivalent) and Rs 33,289 crore, respectively.[3]

While disclosures under the 2016 IDS were Rs 65,250 crore, under the 1997 VDIS Rs 33,289 crore was declared and Rs 9,745 crore of tax was collected at the time. In today's prices, the 1997 revelations would amount to about Rs 82,550 crores, higher than what has been disclosed in 2016.[4]

When compared to GDP, the disclosure in 1997–98 under the VDIS was equivalent to 1.56 per cent of the year's GDP at current prices. The total disclosures in 2015 and 2016 under both the Black Money (Undisclosed Foreign Income and Assets) and Imposition of Tax Act, 2015, and the 2016 IDS were equivalent to 0.51 per cent of GDP at current prices.

However, it must be noted that each scheme had its own features and they cannot be compared. Thus, while collections under the 1997 VDIS were large, the scheme appears to have affected general tax collections that year. Direct tax revenue which had grown by 16 per cent the previous year (1996–97), contracted by 1 per cent net of VDIS collections in 1997–98.

---

[3] Answer to Unstarred Question 2245 in Lok Sabha, 29 July 2016.

[4] Based on a Wholesale Price Index (WPI) of 132.8 (1993–94=100) in 1997–98, and 176 (2004–05=100) in 2015–16, with a linking factor of 1.87 (WPI of 187 [1993–94=100] and 100 [2004–05=100] in 2004–05).

Demonetisation the Next Step?

In the light of the attention that the government has paid to tackling black money from 2014 onwards, it has been argued that the demonetisation of high denomination notes in November 2016 should be seen as the next (major) step in dealing with the black economy. Announcements on the decisions being taken to tackle black money were often accompanied by statements that more was to follow. Changes in rules and regulations, legislative actions tightening existing laws and enacting new ones, the two amnesty schemes on black money and modification of the India-Mauritius DTAA could all be seen as part of a larger commitment to deal with the black economy.

It is, however, also held that the measures taken since 2014 were isolated ones and that therefore demonetisation cannot be seen as the next step in a series of measures for tackling black money. The Budget for 2015–16 announced a list of measures, but the Budget for 2016–17 did not pay the same attention to black money other than announcing a new amnesty scheme. The Prime Minister's speech on 8 November announcing demonetisation did not state that this was part of a larger package and more was to follow. It was a few days later, following widespread criticism that demonetisation by itself was not going to strike at the black economy, that the Prime Minister in another speech announced that demonetisation was to be followed by more measures to deal with generation and holding of illegal funds. It is, therefore, argued that viewed thus, the decision on demonetisation was yet another decision taken in isolation, except that it was of far greater import than any other decision taken by the Narendra Modi government.

— *six* —

Demonetisation 2016

Context and Options

In the speech delivered on the late evening of 8 November 2016, Prime Minister Narendra Modi identified two sets of reasons for the decision to demonetise Rs 500 and Rs 1,000 currency notes:

> For years, this country has felt that corruption, black money and terrorism are festering sores....
>
> ...
>
> To break the grip of corruption and black money, we have decided that the five hundred rupee and thousand rupee currency notes presently in use will no longer be legal tender from midnight tonight.... The five hundred and thousand rupee notes hoarded by anti-national and anti-social elements will become just worthless pieces of paper.[1]

Demonetisation 2016 appears to have been aimed at dealing simultaneously with (i) black money and corruption, and (ii) terrorism financed by counterfeit currency which was the work of 'anti-national' and 'anti-social' elements.

The Gazette Notification of the Department of Economic Affairs of the Ministry of Finance (Number 3407 [E] of 8 November) giving effect to demonetisation, formally noted that following the recommendation of the central board of the RBI,

[1] The full text of the speech is in Annexure I.

> ... whereas, it has been found that fake currency notes of the specified bank notes have been largely in circulation and it has been found to be difficult to easily identify genuine bank notes from the fake ones and that the use of fake currency notes is causing adverse effect to the economy of the country;
>
> And whereas, it has been found that high denomination bank notes are used for storage of unaccounted wealth as has been evident from the large cash recoveries made by law enforcement agencies;
>
> And whereas, it has also been found that fake currency is being used for financing subversive activities such as drug trafficking and terrorism, causing damage to the economy and security of the country and the Central Government after due consideration has decided to implement the recommendations of the Board.[2]

The gazette notification makes no mention of dealing with corruption as one of the reasons for demonetisation. It, in fact, refers to the storage of unaccounted wealth and fake currency, but not corruption.

The 1978 demonetisation of high denominations notes, which was announced on 16 January through an ordinance and not following a recommendation of the RBI board, was effected to end the 'illicit transfer of money for financing transactions'. There was no mention of counterfeit currency in 1978. The preamble to the High Denomination Bank Notes (Demonetisation) Act 1978 states,

> Whereas the availability of high denomination bank notes facilitates the illicit transfer of money for financing transactions which are harmful to the national economy or which are for illegal purposes and it is therefore necessary in the public interest to demonetize high denomination notes.

One should note that legally and technically demonetisation can only address the issue of conterfeit currency. Demonetisation by

[2] The gazette notification is Annexure II.

itself cannot directly deal with cash hoards of black money. It is the information collected during the deposit of old currencies in banks following demonetisation which can be used to unearth unaccounted cash. Those who are unable to launder their illegal hoards or do not want to risk having to explain these stocks during an exchange/deposit at the banks, will, of course, find the value of their hoards extinguished.

Cash in the Black Economy

The effectiveness of demonetisation as an instrument to strike at unaccounted wealth would depend on the extent to which cash is used both to generate black income and to store black wealth. The advantage of using cash in illegal transactions is that it provides for easy conduct of transactions and does not leave any documentary trail that can be traced. Cash is the most anonymous and liquid medium for transactions.

Cash is not the only medium of exchange nor is it the only store of value for black money. Gold is also a medium of exchange and a store of value for black money. Its use, however, is far less important than cash (See chapter 14).

Cash as a Medium of Exchange in the Black Economy

In the domestic economy, the generation and transaction of black money (that is income here) is in both cash and through the banking system.

Small to medium-sized bribes and small to medium-sized transactions not reported to the tax authorities (for example, in retail sales) would almost all be in cash. Large transactions could be partly in cash and partly through the banking system.

Cash is less important in black money in the domestic economy when it is generated in financial markets. In these cases, transactions are through benami bank accounts or through bank transactions not reported to (and not detected by) the tax authorities.

Transactions in black money with the external economy may be cash based or conducted through cross-border financial transactions.

Transactions conducted in the hawala foreign exchange market are likely to be in cash. However, the larger part of black money generated through transactions with the external sector would almost always be through banks which are hidden from the tax authorities (the classic example being under-invoicing of exports and over-invoicing of imports).

Therefore, it is unlikely that transactions in the black economy are more in cash than through the financial system, though the former are more visible and liquid.

Depending on the kind of deal being made, cash may or may not be important for black money transactions, but it is important when a subsequent transaction has to be conducted on the illicit asset.

Cash comes into play when, as discussed in chapter 1, the stock of black money is monetised for a transaction and becomes a flow. For instance, when a stock of gold acquired with unaccounted money is sold, it will be paid for entirely in cash. In other cases, like in sale of real estate acquired in part with unaccounted wealth, the transaction could be partly in cash and partly through the banks.

The value of an asset purchased in part or in full with unaccounted resources depends very much on its liquidity. In many instances, the liquidity of such an asset depends on how easily it can be transacted in cash. If it cannot be easily converted into a flow, the value of the asset will be low. Take the example of a piece of real estate. It may have been acquired with a mixture of accounted and unaccounted funds. Looking to sell it, the seller may also want the sale to be partly with legal funds and partly with black money in cash. Here the availability of a buyer with cash becomes critical for effecting the transaction.

In the intermingling between white and black money that we argued in chapter 1 is a feature of the black economy, cash has an important place. When white money is converted into black money, the medium of transaction is cash. Similarly, when black money is converted into white, by say, entering the banking system, the medium of transaction is again usually cash.

While cash may be an important medium of exchange for black money transactions, to what extent does it serve as an asset for holding black money?

Importance of Cash for Holding Black Money

From the 2012 White Paper's discussion of the factors leading to the generation of black money, the kinds of manipulation of accounts carried out during tax evasion, and the practices in the vulnerable sectors (pp. 3–9 and Annexure IV here), it is possible to develop a typology of sectors/activities where black money is generated and invested. From this typology, one can come to a general understanding of the extent to which cash is used to hold black money in each sector.

1. Illegal activities:
    - 1.1 Smuggling, Extortion
    - 1.2 Trafficking, prostitution
    - 1.3 Corruption
        - 1.3.1 Petty corruption (government servants)
        - 1.3.2 High-level corruption (senior government servants, elected representatives and ministerial representatives)

2. Tax Evasion
    2.1 Unorganised/informal sectors (local trade, petty services, small-scale manufacturing, small-time contract work, and agriculture[3])
    2.2 Organised/corporate sector (mainly in organised trade and real estate, other than through financial sector transactions as in 2.4 and 2.5)
    2.3 Government procurement (local, district, state and central government procurement)
    2.4 Financial Market Transactions (manipulation in stock markets through shell companies)
    2.5 Transactions involving the external sector (over and under-invoicing, transfer pricing, use of innovative derivative investments, etc.)

Each of these sets of activities can see both the generation of black money and its deployment for investment. There are also overlaps. For instance, government procurement could involve corruption and also see the generation of black money through over-invoicing of equipment sales.

There are no substantive surveys or assessment of the black money generated in any of these sectors, and within them the extent of use of cash. It is yet possible to have an idea of the relative importance of cash in each of them, both for transactions and to hold the asset.

First, the criminal activities of trafficking, smuggling and extortion (items 1.1 and 1.2) will almost always involve only cash transactions.

Second, black money generated in petty corruption (1.3.1) and through tax evasion in the unorganised/informal sector (2.1) comes from a numerically very large number of transactions, but

---

[3] Agriculture is not taxed, but when income from non-agricultural activities is clubbed with that from agriculture and is shown as total income from farming, it would be a case of tax evasion.

each transaction involves a relatively small amount, almost all of which will be in cash.

In both sets of cases, cash will dominate transactions, but it would be invested in gold and real estate.

Third, black money from tax evasion in the organised sector can be seen as generated partly through cash (2.2) and partly, perhaps now largely, through the management of books of accounts, and this could be laundered through shell companies or sent abroad through what is called 'trade-based money laundering' (2.4 and 2.5).

Fourth, government procurement (2.3 which would include defence deals) has increased tremendously in the recent decades. Though steps have been taken to make it more transparent, it is accepted that bribe-taking at all levels is significant. Here, cash would dominate at the local level, but reduce in importance as we move up towards procurement contracts of the state/central governments and their agencies.

In both, black money generation in the organised sector and in government procurement, cash may play some role in transactions, but the illicit income earned is invested in assets such as in real estate or in benami bank deposits, at home or abroad.

High-level corruption (item 1.3.2) would involve payments abroad through financial transactions or when done locally, partly in cash, it is then quickly invested in benami assets. Where elected representatives are involved, some of these assets are presumably liquidated ahead of the elections to generate the necessary cash.

Fifth, the big change in recent decades should be in the growth of tax evasion in domestic financial market transactions and in activities involving the external sector (items 2.4 and 2.5; at times the two are connected).

Large value transactions in the financial market and elsewhere that escape the tax net take place through fake book entries and even through formal channels of financial institutons. This black money is then invested in assets, also through transactions conducted through the banking system.

From the above, it would seem that, on balance, while cash remains important as a medium of exchange for black money, it is not so as a store of value of black money. The illicit income earned is invested in assets such as gold and real estate, or laundered through dummy companies or even placed in benami bank accounts.

Large black incomes are also siphoned out of the country and held in assets/bank accounts there, only to be used subsequently for round-tripping and invested in India in equity or real estate when the opportunity arises.

Select statistics on seizures during income tax raids in the country presented in the White Paper show that the assets seized in select years are barely 10 per cent of undeclared incomes (Table 6.1), suggesting that much of the assets built-up from undeclared incomes are successfully hidden from the eyes of the law. Cash as a proportion of the undeclared incomes is between 1.75 per cent and 7.3 per cent.

TABLE 6.1: Distribution of Assets Seized By Type in Select Income Tax Seizures

Financial Year	*No. of Warrants Executed*	*Value of Assets Seized (In Rs Crore)*				*Total Undisclosed Income Admitted (In Rs Crore)*
		Cash	*Jewellery*	*Other Assets*	*Total*	
2006–07	3,534	187.48	99.19	77.96	364.64	3,612.89
2007–08	3,281	206.35	128.07	93.39	427.82	4,160.58
2008–09	3,379	339.86	122.18	88.19	550.23	4,613.06
2009–10	3,454	300.97	132.2	530.33	963.5	8,101.35
2010–11	4,852	440.28	184.15	150.55	774.98	10,649.16
2011–12	5,260	499.91	271.4	134.3	905.61	9,289.43

Source: Table 4.4 reproduced from page 47 of 2012 White Paper.

Thus, prima facie, cash is not a dominant component of the aggregate stock of black money or of the total value of transactions in the black economy. Yet, attacking the cash component of black money on a priority basis can be justified on two counts.

First, because cash is the one instrument which is used for both transactions and investment—more for the former than for the latter—an attack on 'black cash', as it were, could have a disruptive effect on the market value of the stocks in the black economy. Second, attacking cash may be the most effective way of communicating the government's determination to deal with the black economy. So any attempt to disable its use may send the appropriate signals to the holders of unaccounted wealth and to people at large.

Demonetisation as One of the Options

The 2012 White Paper noted,

> ... the primary importance of cash in relation to both generation and use of black money. However, given the primary importance of cash in relation to both generation and use of black money, there is no alternative but to target cash transactions in a way that will not affect those complying with the law, while making it difficult for those intending to generate and utilise black money. (p. 55)

It is possible to support the contention of the White Paper that cash is of primary importance in relation to the black economy. Though as mentioned earlier, cash is not a dominant part of the black economy, it lends liquidity to the transactions in the black economy.

The contention that there is no alternative but to target cash transactions may be acceptable provided it is recognised that it may be a necessary, but not a sufficient condition for a successful attack on the black economy.

The observation of the White Paper that the target should be cash transactions is also conditional, namely it should be done 'in a way that will not affect those complying with the law'. The option of demonetisation to deal with black money does not conform to this requirement and is thus inconsistent with the White Paper.

It is, therefore, essential to explore alternative ways in which the hardship to the larger population can be reduced.

For instance, close monitoring of cash withdrawals at the bank branch level is one option. Since all cash originates in the banking system, there will be information on which banks, branches and accounts from which cash is withdrawn. Once the location of large cash withdrawals in, say the last five years, has been identified and then followed up by an examination of the withdrawals at the identified branches, substantial information will become available to the tax authorities. This information can then be used to track down the holders of accounts seeing large cash withdrawals.

The interface with the authorities in this alternative approach, in contrast to that in demonetisation, will be confined to a small population. Targeting the few who could potentially be guilty rather than the mass of innocents is rational and minimises the cost for the people and the government as well.

COUNTERFEIT CURRENCY

Demonetisation is well-recognised as an effective instrument to deal with counterfeit currency.

It is appropriate to accept that the problem of counterfeiting was serious enough for the government to adopt steps to demonetise high value currency. (See the Appendix to this chapter for a discussion of estimates of counterfeit currency in India).

If counterfeiting was the main issue underlying the need to demonetise high value currency, then the time given for the process of demonetisation could have been long enough to minimise the inconvenience and hardship caused to people. The design of the Demonetisation 2016, however, seems to indicate that the major objective was to attack black money rather than counterfeit currency.

In the past, the RBI has carried out a phased withdrawal of currency smoothly.

In January 2014, the central bank announced that it was withdrawing from circulation all pre-2005 currency notes and that they would cease to be legal tender after 31 March 2014. The RBI later progressively extended the deadline to June 2016. The currencies continued to be legal tender during this process and thereafter. The reason given for the withdrawal was that the pre-2005 series had fewer security features than the post-2005 series. The process was conducted in an orderly fashion and there was little panic among the public.

The question then is why a similar process could not have been carried out in late 2016 as well, if counterfeit currency was the main concern that had to be dealt with. If currency with newer security features had to be introduced, then the older series could have been withdrawn over a period of time, with the banks replacing the old with the new, even as the old currency notes continued to be legal tender.

SUMMING-UP

To sum up, combining the objectives of dealing with counterfeit currency and black money in Demonetisation 2016 resulted in a design, which, in order to entrap a small number of suspects who hoarded black money in cash, ended up hurting a much larger number of honest people. This was despite the awareness of the problem of following such an approach which was articulated in the White Paper placed before Parliament in 2012.

Appendix

Estimate of Counterfeit Currency

Assessing the extent of counterfeit currency in circulation is difficult because of the limited nature of information available in the public domain.

The data available is the number of counterfeits detected/recovered in the banking system, including in the currency note processing system of the RBI, which is published regularly in the *RBI Annual Reports*. From this data, one can arrive at the aggregate number of counterfeit notes which have been detected and reported (Table 6A.1).

During 2008–09, aggregate detection more than doubled (103.3 per cent) to 398,111. It may be noted that during 2008–09, notes in circulation increased by 10.7 per cent while counterfeit notes detected in the banking channel increased by 103.3 per cent. Growth in counterfeit currency detected has, however, moderated in recent years.

By more closely examining the data on counterfeiting reported through the banking channel, one can assess the incidence of counterfeiting to some extent.

For example, if it is assumed that counterfeiting is more prevalent in notes of Rs 100 and above (a rational assumption), then its incidence could go up almost threefold—from 6 to 7 pieces per million to 17 to 18 pieces per million (Row 5 in Table 6A.1). This ratio is even higher if we assume that most of the counterfeit notes were in the high denomination Rs 500 and Rs 1,000 denominations. For some years, the incidence of counterfeiting is as high as 100 per million pieces (Row 6). Therefore, while the published data as disseminated by the RBI shows a low average percentage of counterfeits, the effective level of counterfeiting—which in all likelihood is concentrated in Rs 500 and Rs 1,000 notes—is much larger.

These numbers could still be an underestimate of the extent of detection. Banks are expected to report statistics of fake currency detected at all their branches to the RBI on a regular basis. But customers may be reluctant to report the counterfeit notes even if they discover them. There is no disincentive to bring them to the notice of the banks.

Table 6A.1: Counterfeit Currency Notes Detected in the Banking System

Items	*2007–08*	*2008–09*	*2009–10*	*2010–11*	*2011–12*	*2012–13*	*2013–14*	*2014–15*	*2015–16*
1. Notes in circulation (million pieces)	44,225 (11.0)	48,963 (10.7)	56,549 (15.5)	64,577 (14.2)	69,382 (7.4)	73,517 (6.0)	77,330 (5.2)	83,579 (8.1)	90,266 (8.0)
2. Notes in circulation of high denomination (Rs 100 and above) (million pieces)	20,131 (2.0)	21,788 (8.2)	23,509 (7.9)	25,957 (10.4)	27,844 (7.2)	29,439 (5.7)	31,251 (6.2)	33,766 (8.0)	37,811 (12.0)
3. Notes in circulation of higher denomination (Rs 500 and above) (million pieces)	2,824 (50.7)	3,836 (35.8)	4,766 (24.2)	6,054 (27.0)	6,938 (14.6)	8,598 (23.9)	10,162 (18.2)	11,224 (10.5)	12,652 (12.7)
4. Counterfeit notes detected (no. of pieces)	195,811 (86.9)	398,111 (103.3)	401,476 (0.8)	435,607 (8.5)	521,155 (19.6)	498,252 (–4.4)	488,273 (–2.0)	594,446 (21.7)	632,926 (6.5)
5. Counterfeit notes per million NIC [(4)/(1)]	4.4	8.1	7.1	6.7	7.5	6.8	6.3	7.1	7.0
6. Counterfeit notes *vis-à-vis* per million of high denominated notes [(4)/(2)]	9.7	18.3	17.1	16.8	18.2	16.9	15.6	17.6	16.7
7. Counterfeit notes *vis-à-vis* per million of higher denominated notes [(4)/(3)]	69.3	103.8	84.2	72.0	75.1	57.9	48.0	53.0	50.0

Note: Figures in parentheses are year-on-year growth in percentage terms.
Source: *RBI Annual Report*, various years.

RBI reports do not publish estimates of the counterfeit currency in circulation. However, the Rajya Sabha was informed in August 2016 that a study conducted by the Indian Statistical Institute, Kolkata under the overall supervision of the National Investigation Agency (NIA) had estimated that the face value of the fake currency notes in circulation was Rs 400 crore and that this had remained constant the previous four years.

Irrespective of the magnitudes, demonetisation of specific series may be warranted if the security features have been broken in a significant manner. Such actions would be specific to the series.

— *seven* —

Demonetisation 2016

Design and Implementation

India's mammoth demonetisation in 2016 needs to be assessed in the first instance in terms of its design and then of implementation.

Design

There are two important areas in the design of India's demonetisation exercise that require analysis. First, the scale of demonetisation, and, second, the time-frame for the completion of the process. There is also a third and less important issue which has been expressed in the media about the features of the new currency issued by the RBI

Scale

The central government took a decision to demonetise the Rs 500 and Rs 1,000 currency notes in circulation, and introduce a new currency of Rs 2,000 denomination and a new series of Rs 500 currency.

The Rs 500 and Rs 1,000 notes accounted for 86 per cent of the value of currency in circulation as of March 2016. The Rs 500 notes accounted for 47.6 per cent and the Rs 1,000 notes for 38.4 per cent of the value of the notes in circulation.[1] (See the appendix to this chapter for an examination of the growth in high denomination notes over the years.) Removal of this currency would have to be accompanied by the reintroduction of a currency of a new series of the same order of magnitude.

Demonetisation on such an enormous scale taking out more than 86 per cent of the currency and then introducing a new currency is a huge operation with immense challenges.

Scale: Withdrawal of Currency

Table 7.1 gives the distribution of currencies as of 31 March 2016.

To make an assessment if the demonetised currencies were of high value, researchers have compared the per capita income in 2016 with the face value of the currency notes which have been demonetised, and compared these values with the 1978 demonetisation exercise when Rs 10,000, Rs 5,000 and Rs 1,000 notes were rendered invalid tender.[2]

The higher the ratio of the per capita income to the value of the currency note, the more likely it is that the currency will be used in everyday transactions. Conversely, the lower the ratio, the more likely the currency notes are used only by a small number of people and would be the preferred form for hoarding cash.

In 1977–78, the per capita income at current prices for the year was Rs 1,642. The per capita income that year as a mutliple

---

[1] By 8 November 2016, the numbers and proportions had grown. On that day, there were 17,165 million pieces of the Rs 500 currency and 6,858 million pieces of the Rs 1,000 currency, totalling to a value of Rs 15,440.5 billion (Lok Sabha unstarred question number 2949 (2 December 2016). According to the *RBI Weekly Statistical Supplement*, the value of all notes in circulation as of 4 November 2016, was Rs 17,644.86 billion. So the high denomination notes demonetised constituted around 87.5 per cent of the notes in circulation on 8 November 2016.

[2] The analysis here is based on that carried out by Nag (2016).

of the value of the Rs 10,000, Rs 5,000 and Rs 1,000 notes works out to be 0.16, 0.33 and 1.6, respectively. In 2016, the ratios were much higher. In 2016, when the annual per capita income at current prices was Rs 93,231[3], the income–value of the currency ratio was 93.2 for the Rs 1,000 note and as much as 186.4 for the Rs 500 note.

TABLE 7.1: Banknotes in Circulation

Denomination (Rs)	*Volume (million pieces)*			*Value (Rs bn)*		
	Mar-14	*Mar-15*	*Mar-16*	*Mar-14*	*Mar-15*	*Mar-16*
1	2	3	4	5	6	7
2 and 5	11,698	11,672	11,626	46	46	45
	(15.1)	(13.9)	(12.9)	(0.4)	(0.3)	(0.3)
10	26,648	30,304	32,015	266	303	320
	(34.5)	(36.3)	(35.5)	(2.1)	(2.1)	(1.9)
20	4,285	4,350	4,924	86	87	98
	(5.5)	(5.2)	(5.4)	(0.7)	(0.6)	(0.6)
50	3,448	3,487	3,890	172	174	194
	(4.5)	(4.2)	(4.3)	(1.3)	(1.2)	(1.2)
100	14,765	15,026	15,778	1,476	1,503	1,578
	(19.1)	(18.0)	(17.5)	(11.5)	(10.5)	(9.6)
500	11,405	13,128	15,707	5,702	6,564	7,854
	(14.7)	(15.7)	(17.4)	(44.4)	(46.0)	(47.8)
1,000	5,081	5,612	6,326	5,081	5,612	6,326
	(6.6)	(6.7)	(7.0)	(39.6)	(39.3)	(38.6)
Total	77,330	83,579	90,266	12,829	14,289	16,415

Note: Figures in parentheses represent the percentage share in total.
Source: Table VIII.1 reproduced from *Annual Report of the Reserve Bank of India 2015–16.*

[3] Per capita income figures from *Economic Survey 2015–16*; figure for 2015–16 is an advance estimate for the year.

Clearly, when compared to 1978, the high value currencies demonetised in 2016 were of lower value in relation to the per capita income.

In 1978, even the Rs 1,000 note (the smallest currency to be demonetised at the time) could be said to have been of high value, but in 2016 the Rs 1,000 and Rs 500 notes—especially the former—were far from possessing a very high purchasing power when compared to the per capita income.

It is, therefore, more than likely that in 2016 a very large proportion of the high denomination notes—especially the Rs 500 notes—was being used for everyday legal transactions.

If the Rs 500 currency note was of common use in the economy, then any demonetisation of this currency aimed at the holders of black money in these notes was also going to hurt the much larger population which was earning its income legally and using this currency for legal transactions.

For this and other related reasons, a 2012 Ministry of Finance Committee on measures to tackle black money, which was headed by the Chairman of the Central Board of Direct Taxes, did not view the option of demonetisation of high denomination currency with favour:

> In India, demonetization was implemented in 1946 and 1978. Experts have criticized that demonetization did not achieve the objective it was aimed at. Further, inflation over the years and a large cash economy requires higher denomination currency notes to keep the cost of monetary management of the economy low. (pp. 12–13)

Alternatives

It is possible to think of three other options within demonetisation.

(1) One option was to restrict demonetisation to the Rs 1,000 note. This would have limited the withdrawal of currency

to 38.4 per cent of cash in circulation and, therefore, caused less dislocation.

(2) The second option was to demonetise both currencies, but to do so sequentially, first demonetise the Rs 1,000 note (38.4 per cent of the currency in circulation), and then the Rs 500 note (48.6 per cent of the currency).

Either option would have served the purpose of ending the circulation of counterfeit currency (of the Rs 1,000 note in the first case and of both the Rs 1,000 and Rs 500 notes in the second). Both options would also have served to provide information on the black money held as cash, less in the first option and more in the second option.

The effectiveness of the first option (demonetising only the Rs 1,000 note) to uncover black money held in cash would depend on the assumption that a larger part of the illegal cash hoard was held in Rs 1,000 and not Rs 500 notes. There is no information to suggest the correctness or otherwise of this assumption, though inflation may have worked to shift illegal holdings of cash over time in favour of the Rs 1,000 notes.

In choosing between these two options, the critical trade-off is between minimising the inconvenience to people and maximising the effectiveness of the decision from the point of view of unearthing black money.

There was also a third option.

(3) Demonetisation could have been implemented over a period of time, with the currencies to be withdrawn remaining valid tender during this period for all transactions. This would have permitted holders of the demonetised currency to exchange them at banks in an orderly manner, and not have to crowd the banks. The counterfeit currency would have been identified during the exchange. To unearth black money, a tax amnesty could have been announced

at the same time. The amnesty scheme would have run during the period of demonetisation.

There is a case for and against this particular option. The case for is, of course, that there would have been negligible inconvenience to the public. The case against is that all holders of unaccounted cash may not have declared their black money under the amnesty scheme. Some would have used the window to launder their black money into white.

Scale: Introduction of New Currency

The second aspect of the scale of the demonetisation process is the design for the process of replacing the cash that was withdrawn.

When 86 per cent of the currency in circulation is to be invalidated in a cash-dependent economy, the reintroduction of cash has to be planned to the minutest detail in order to minimise the disruption, especially for those who had no alternative to using cash.

This needs to take into account: (i) the type of currencies to be introduced, (ii) the time taken to reinject cash into the economy and (iii) the logistics of the process.

Currency management by the RBI is described and discussed in chapter 11. Here a brief overview of the issues relating to reintroduction of cash is presented.

Type of Currency

The demonetisation of the two highest currency notes was accompanied by the introduction of a new series of Rs 500 notes and the currency of an even higher denomination—the Rs 2,000 currency note.

It may have been a strange decision to take to introduce a new currency of even higher denomination, given that one of the objectives of the entire exercise was to remove high denomination notes from circulation. The introduction of the Rs 2,000 note was obviously meant to hasten the process of 'remonetisation' of the economy—increasing the value of currency in circulation which had been reduced to 14 per cent of the level on 8 November. It is also likely that over time the stock of Rs 2,000 notes in circulation will be gradually brought down by winding down the printing of this particular currency.

Time Period for Injection of Cash

A close analysis of the challenges the RBI faced in introducing cash to replace the demonetised currency is presented in the Section 'In the Aftermath of the Announcement' (pp. 149–151) of Chapter 11. The broad conclusions are below.

The removal of 86 per cent of the currency in circulation requires quick injection of replacement cash.

The time to be taken depends on: (i) the capacity of the printing presses to meet the new and very large additional demand over and above the routine requirement, (ii) the availability of paper and ink, (iii) the option to supplement domestic printing of notes with supplies from abroad, which in turn would depend on the availability of spare capacity.

The demonetisation of 22,033 million notes of Rs 500 and Rs 1,000 denominations meant that the currency of equivalent value or close to that value (Rs 14.18 lakh crore or trillion) had to be replaced quickly. However, the capacity of the domestic printing presses is meant to cater to an annual indent by the RBI to meet routine annual increases, which in recent years amounted to 22,000 million pieces of *all* denominations. This implies that what the printing presses normally print in a year, they had to print in a few weeks.

The introduction of the Rs 2,000 note and making presses work an extra shift was no doubt of help, but obviously grossly inadequate to meet the requirement in a timely manner. While it is possible to contract foreign presses to print currency for India, the available capacity world wide would normally be limited and pre-committed for other needs and may not have been available at a short notice to meet India's needs even in part.

Cash lines at ATMs and banks continued through November and into December 2016, indicating the absence of cash. Banks were also making available cash at less than the promised limits. Both caused immense hardship to the honest citizen who only sought to draw on savings/earnings that were legitimately hers/his.

Many independent estimates were made of the time that would be taken before a semblance of normalcy returned in terms of cash in circulation. Some suggested that it would be January 2017 before the shortage eased; and yet others suggested it would be February 2017.

In other words, it was always obvious that the replacement would take at least two months. This is, by all accounts, too long a period for the workers, self-employed and the employers who are dependent on cash for their daily legal transactions.

Absence of Notice for Demonetisation

The prepartions for demonetisation were conducted in secret and the announcment was sudden.

Secrecy would be seen as necessary in a major drive against a black economy. This is because the powerful forces in the black economy would otherwise be able to escape detection, and simultaneously take steps to hide their black wealth, either by spiriting it out of the country or laundering it to make it legal. There can also be arguments against a sudden and surprise announcement. The 1978 demonetisation exercise—also aimed at unearthing black money—was announced and then put into effect six weeks later. None of the demonetisation exercises carried out elsewhere in the world in the recent decades—in Russia,

Myanmar and Zimbabwe—were done with secrecy, though these were done to deal with a debased currency rather than to unearth illegal hoards. In these countries, demonetisation was announced ahead of the date for formal completion of the process with the currency remaining legal tender during the intervening period.[4]

Obviously, secrecy was needed mainly to subserve the objective of tackling the cash element of black money; and was not integral to demonetisation per se. If time were given, the holders of illegal wealth would, of course, have sought to use this period to convert these cash hoards into other assets at home or outside the country. It is now evident that in the end this is what happened even after currencies were demonetisation at one stroke.

Holders of unaccounted wealth in cash were able to find ways to make this cash enter the legal banking system. This defeated one purpose of the demonetisation exercise. However, the entry into the formal banking system of this cash hoards has brought this part of black money into the legal and white economy. So, the dissolution of this segment of black wealth can be seen as a positive development, even if the holders of what was black money may have for now escaped detection (pending examination of large deposits by the income tax authorities).

Within three weeks of the November demonetisation, the government launched a new amnesty scheme, the PMGKY. This scheme came within a few months of the Income Disclosure Scheme 2016, which was operational before demonetisation of the high denomination notes was announced.

Under the second amnesty scheme of the year, which would run until 31 March 2017, those who declared unaccounted income/wealth would pay 50 per cent tax, and maintain 25 per cent of the declared income/wealth in interest-free deposits for four years.

---

[4] An exception would be the December 2016 demonetisation of the Venezuelan 100 Bolivar which was later given an extended period for the currency withdrawal.

Four possible objectives of this new PMGKY can be inferred: (i) to encourage voluntary disclosure of black money by those who did not come forward during a similar amnesty scheme earlier in 2016, (ii) to bring black money into the banking system and thereby make it part of the formal and legal system, (iii) to provide a direct fiscal gain via payment of the 50 per cent tax and (iv) to provide the GoI with compulsory interest-free deposits (which the state governments would not have access to).

IMPLEMENTATION

There have been many questions about the manner in which demonetisation has been effected.

Legality

There has been a clutch of petitions in the high courts and Supreme Court questioning the legality of the demonetisation process. These have been seen as organised around two broad areas.[5] The first is the legality of demonetisation by notification under Section 26(2) of the RBI Act of 34, unlike on the two previous occasions in 1946 and 1978 when it was carried out under an ordinance which was subsequently converted into a law. The second set of issues under which Demonetisation 2016 has been questioned is whether it violates the right to property. While the courts are yet (February 2017) to deliver their judgments, it does seem on balance that there is not much legal basis to question Demonetisation 2016.

A more serious issue is that relating to adherence to the spirit of the law. It has been argued that the 'chaotic and misguided' pronouncements during the first month after demonetisation when

---

[5] The first half of the brief discussion here is based largely on Kumar (2016).

decisions on cash withdrawal limits/cash deposits/continued use of the Rs 500 and Rs 1,000 notes were modified on a day-to-day basis amounted to a lack of adherence to the spirit of the law and weakened the citizen's faith in the government's ability to adhere to this spirit of the law.

Yet another important area in which the implementation of the demonetisation process has come to be questioned is whether the strict controls on the amount of cash a citizen can withdraw from her own savings and then the RBI's frequent inability to deliver on even these limited commitments constitute an abridgement of the fundamental rights guaranteed by the Constitution.

The scheme was amended and changed more than 50 times between 8 November and 15 December (This is discussed in detail further in the Section 'Lack of Planning and Co-ordination'). The first set of announcements on cash availability at banks and ATMs carry an implied promise to maintain them so that the public may cope with the overnight withdrawal of legal tender in their hands. Limiting these limited rights can constitute a breach of such promise, and certainly a breach of legitimate expectations of governmental obligations. The need for overnight action does not free the government from its duty to limit the negative fallout; on the contrary it imposes a duty of care which is higher than what normally can be expected. The almost casual manner in which announcements and arrangements were made, changed, withdrawn and freshly imposed in November and December 2016 hardly measure up to sound management.

Deprival of money, even in the short term, affects the right to livelihood under Article 21, especially of the marginalised sections who are dependent on the cash structure of the economy. It would also affect several of the rights guaranteed by Article 19, including trade and business, and movement. State action can be justified only if it can pass multiple tests—that the restrictions are necessary, that they are reasonable, that they are not arbitrary, and that the doctrine of proportionality is not breached. Both ends and means must pass legal scrutiny.

In considering the legality of the measures that were taken, it would be relevant to see what other measures are taken or not taken to achieve the stated ends. If other relevant and necessary measures were not taken, then it is difficult to justify curbs on common citizens.

Planning and Co-ordination

Since secrecy was given paramount importance, consultations could not be conducted in a wide circle. This inevitably resulted in administrative difficulties in critical processes. Yet, the most striking event which had serious consequences for the ability to conduct cash transactions after the November demonetisation was the initial failure of the ATMs to dispense Rs 2,000 currency notes.

When the decision was taken to modify the sizes of both the new Rs 2,000 currency note and the new series of the Rs 500 currency note, it was not realised that there would be a need to recalibrate the ATMs if they were to dispense the new notes. It is surprising that such a simple matter appears not to have been thought of.

It took until the end of November 2016 for most of the 215,000 ATMs in the country to be recalibrated to dispense the new Rs 2,000 notes.

Changing Regulations

In a major exercise for which there is no prior experience, there is bound to be a need to modify rules and regulations based on developments on the ground. Such changes should be seen as the administration responding to the ground reality, and the RBI/government cannot be entirely faulted for the many changes made in the regulations week after week.

However, a frequent change in the rules regarding access to cash and for exchange of the demonetised currencies induces uncertainties and tends to confuse people and therefore results in unnecessary hardship.

The rules on ceilings on withdrawals from ATMs were changed thrice after demonetisation was announced on 8 November 2016. The rules on the over-the-counter exchange of old notes at banks by individuals were also changed twice (the limits were increased and then halved) between 8 November 2016 and 24 November 2016 before it was disallowed altogether, though the earlier deadline had been given as 30 December 2016.

The Finance Minister appealed in mid-November 2016 to the public not to crowd the banks to deposit their cash since there was time until the end of December to do so. Yet, in mid-December, the RBI suddenly announced that (i) depositors could not make more than one deposit of Rs 5,000, (ii) depositors would have to explain why they had delayed making deposits, (iii) those depositing more than Rs 5,000 would have to explain to two bank officers the reasons for the 'delay'. Following a storm of protests, the RBI modified these rules within a day and allowed 'Know Your Customer (KYC)-compliant' customers to make Rs 5,000+ deposits without any hindrance.

The lack of planning for cash replacement also meant that even six weeks after demonetisation (mid-December 2016), it was an exception rather than the rule that (i) ATMs could dispense the promised amount of Rs 2,500 a week, and (ii) that banks could offer savings account holders the promised Rs 24,000 of cash withdrawal by cheque every week.

All these changes were aimed at preventing holders of black money laundering their funds through the banking system. What they did though was to presume that everyone was guilty and make it extremely difficult for law-abiding citizens to deposit their legitimate savings in banks.

Insensitivity

There was also an occasional lack of insensitivity on the part of the public authorities, such as in their suggestion soon after demonetisation for the public to use digital instruments to carry out their monetary transactions.

Those who had access to digital instruments such as credit cards, e-wallets and online bank transfer facilities, did use these instruments with increasing frequency. Those in difficulty and most in need of cash were, however, those without any access to digital instruments.

Status

The initial expectations were that upto Rs 3–4 lakh crore (trillion) of the Rs 14.1 lakh crore (trillion) of high denomination notes in circulation (March 2016) would not be declared and would, therefore, constitute unaccounted cash/wealth that would lose value. Official figures on the currency swap until 10 December 2016 had shown that Rs 12.44 lakh crore (trillion) had already been exchanged or deposited in banks. At the time of writing (mid-February 2017), official figures from the RBI about the total value of the demonetised currencies deposited in the banks or exchanged up to 31 December 2016 were not available. However, various media reports stated that almost the entire stock of high denomination notes had made its way back into the banking system by 30 December 2016.

Summing-Up

There is a view that to be effective, a decision to render invalid particular currency notes in order to flush out black money has to be a closely guarded secret. That it was, therefore, inevitable that there were missteps on the way to Demonetisation 2016. On the same lines, it is also argued that it is necessary to keep changing the rules and regulations to keep ahead of the holders of black money since these powerful forces keep making every effort to launder their black money and escape the tax net.

However, for the public—an overwhelming number of whom were honest citizens—trying to cope with the hardship, everything about India's 2016 demonetisation exercise left them with the deeply uncomfortable feeling that there was a lack of careful thought and detailed planning ahead of the demonetisation announcement. In the eagerness to snare the holders of black money, deep pain was inflicted on the much larger population of honest citizens.

Appendix

Growth of High Denomination Notes

After the announcement of demonetisation, one of the issues commented on was the growth of cash of high denomination notes, in particular, in the recent years.

Tables 7A.1, 7A.2 and 7A.3 give some numbers about the high denomination notes, the growth in GDP (current prices) and the currency–GDP ratio. (These tables have been extracted and extended from Tables 1, 3 and 5 from Rajakumar and Shetty [2016].)[6]

Table 7A.1: Value of High Denomination Notes in Value of All Notes in Circulation (in %)

	Share of Rs 500 notes	*Share of Rs 1,000 notes*	*HDNs in Total*
2000–01	24.9	1.8	26.7
2001–02	28.0	2.9	30.9
2002–03	34.1	5.8	39.9
2003–04	38.4	8.6	47.0
2004–05	42.3	11.6	53.9
2005–06	43.2	15.3	58.5
2006–07	45.4	18.9	64.3
2007–08	45.2	24.3	69.5
2008–09	45.3	28.2	73.4
2009–10	46.2	30.2	76.5
2010–11	47.6	32.3	79.9
2011–12	48.7	32.9	81.7
2012–13	46.0	36.9	82.9

(Contd)

[6] We are grateful to J. Dennis Rajakumar and the EPW Research Foundation for giving us the relevant data and extending the series for Tables 7A.1–3 here.

Table 7A.1 (Contd)

	Share of Rs 500 notes	*Share of Rs 1,000 notes*	*HDNs in Total*
2013–14	44.4	39.6	84.0
2014–15	45.9	39.3	85.2
2015–16	47.8	38.5	86.4

Source: Based on data extracted from RBI (2016), *Handbook of Statistics on Indian Economy 2015–16*.

Table 7A.2: Growth Rates of HDNs, Total Bank Notes and GDP (%)

	HDNs	*Total Bank Notes*	*GDP (Current)*
GDP 2004–05 series			
2001–02	33.6	15.2	8.2
2002–03	45.0	12.4	7.7
2003–04	**37.0**	**16.2**	**12.0**
2004–05	**29.5**	**13.0**	**14.1**
2005–06	**26.6**	**16.8**	**13.9**
2006–07	29.3	17.6	16.3
2007–08	26.7	17.2	16.1
2008–09	**23.7**	**17.1**	**12.9**
2009–10	**20.5**	**15.7**	**15.1**
2010–11	**24.1**	**18.7**	**20.2**
2011–12	14.9	12.5	15.7
2012–13	12.3	10.6	12.2
GDP 2012 series			
2012–13	12.3	10.6	13.9
2013–14	**11.7**	**10.2**	**13.3**
2014–15	**12.9**	**11.4**	**10.8**
2015–16	**16.5**	**14.9**	**8.7**

Source: Same as Table 7A.1.

TABLE 7A.3: Total Bank Notes and GDP

	Total Bank Notes (Rs in Billion)	*GDP (Rs in Billion)*	*Total Bank Notes as % of GDP*
GDP 2004–05 series			
2000–01	2,125	21,774	9.8
2001–02	2,447	23,558	10.4
2002–03	2,751	25,363	10.8
2003–04	3,198	28,415	11.3
2004–05	3,612	32,422	11.1
2005–06	4,219	36,934	11.4
2006–07	4,961	42,947	11.6
2007–08	5,816	49,871	11.7
2008–09	6,811	56,301	12.1
2009–10	7,883	64,778	12.2
2010–11	9,359	77,841	12.0
2011–12	10,528	90,097	11.7
2012–13	11,647	101,133	11.5
GDP 2012 series			
2011–12	10,528	87,360	12.1
2012–13	11,647	99,513	11.7
2013–14	12,831	112,728	11.4
2014–15	14,289	124,882	11.4
2015–16	16,416	135,761	12.1

GDP refers to gross domestic product at current and market price.

Source: Based on data extracted from RBI (2016a), *Handbook of Statistics on Indian Economy 2015–16.*

One can point out, firstly, that there has been a steady growth since the early 2000s in the share of the value of both the high denomination notes (HDNs) in the total value of notes in circulation (Table 7A.1). There are no unusual patterns. There are only yearly increases of varying magnitudes.

There seem to be no links either between the growth in currency and the conduct of national elections. Parliamentary elections were held in

April–May 2004, April–May 2009 and again in April–May 2014. There is no spurt ahead of and during the financial years in which elections were held and no decline the next financial year, as one would expect if the HDNs are drawn in disproportionately large numbers ahead of and during the election year (growth rates highlighted in Table 7A.1). So, there must be some doubts about the view that years of elections see a spurt in the HDNs in circulation.

Second, the value of HDNs in circulation has been increasing faster than all notes in circulation (Table 7A.2). But their growth seems broadly in line with growth in nominal GDP.

Third, since the early 2000s, there has been a modest rise in the currency-GDP ratio (Table 7A.3), the reasons for which we do not know.

— *eight* —

Promotion of a 'Less-Cash' Economy

The acute cash shortage that followed the demonetisation of 86 per cent of the currency in circulation prompted the government to advocate and accelerate digitalisation of payments. To overcome the shortage of currency, the RBI too advised the public to adopt electronic/digital forms to execute transactions.

As the process of demonetisation progressed, attention was also paid to the formalisation of the informal, that is, on bringing the informal sector into the formal sector. It is believed that one way in which the informal can be brought into the formal is through digitalisation, or by minimising the use of cash. This discourse on 'formalisation of the informal' was based on the questionable assumption that the informal sector was an important source of black money generation.

The Prime Minister's speech on 8 November 2016 announcing demonetisation did not mention the need to accelerate the shift to electronic/digital payments as one of the main or secondary objectives. The gazette notification on demonetisation also did not refer to the need to promote digitalisation of the economy, nor reduce the use of cash in the economy.

Later, commentators noted that the Prime Minister had begun paying attention to digitalisation in his speeches.

It is obvious that the overarching consideration in the discussions and policy measures on digitalisation after demonetisation was announced has been to wean the economy away from cash so that the scope for transactions outside the gaze of the tax authorities can be reduced. This is derived from the belief that the larger part of black money transactions takes place in cash. But as explained in the earlier chapters, such transactions take place both in cash and through the financial system, and both within India and across borders.

Digitalisation of monetary transaction has been in progress for more than a decade now. The new impetus to digitalisation after demonetisation should, therefore, be viewed in the broader context.

CASH IN THE INDIAN ECONOMY

The popular impression is that the use of cash in India is very high. However, the cash-GDP ratio in India is not exceptionally high when compared with the other developing countries or even with some of the advanced countries.

Inter-country statistics compiled by the Bank of International Settlements (BIS) for a select group of countries indicate that the cash-GDP ratio in India is not too far off the average and lower than in some advanced economies.

In 2015, India's currency-GDP ratio was 12.2 per cent compared to the 9 per cent average for the select countries (Table 8.1). For a number of large advanced countries, the percentage is around this mark or even higher: 10.6 per cent for the European Union (EU), 11.8 per cent for Switzerland, 15.5 per cent for Hong Kong and as much as 20.7 per cent for Japan.

It should be noted that there is no one-to-one relationship between per capita income and the cash-GDP ratio. Switzerland, the richest country in the group, has one of the highest cash-GDP ratios in the group, while South Africa, the country with the second lowest GDP per capita has, after Sweden, the lowest cash-GDP ratio.

TABLE 8.1: Per capita GDP and Currency in Circulation as Percentage of GDP

Country	*GDP per capita ($)*	*Currency as percentage of GDP*
	2015	2015
Switzerland	80,950	11.76
United States	56,215	7.9
Singapore	52,890	9.55
Australia	51,041	4.64
Sweden	50,313	1.73
United Kingdom	43,805	3.72
Canada	43,475	4.08
Hong Kong SAR	42,214	15.51
Japan	32,436	20.66
Korea	27,214	5.56
Saudi Arabia	20,828	8.2
Mexico	9,510	6.83
Turkey	9,121	5.37
Russia	9,098	10.56
Brazil	8,649	3.82
South Africa	5,801	2.39
India	**1,651**	**12.25**
Euro area		10.63
Average	32,071	9

Source: Extracted from BIS, 'Statistics on Payment, Clearing and Settlement Systems', tables 1 and 2, available at http://www.bis.org/cpmi/publ/d155.htm, accessed on 3 December 2016.

The cash-GDP ratio is a summary figure. Surveys by market research and other agencies of consumer transactions in India indicate a very high dependence on cash for transactions by consumers.

A 2013 analysis by the card merchant MasterCard indicated that in India as much of 98 per cent of consumer transactions by volume were in cash, and as much as 68 per cent in value.[1] In a group of 10 advanced and large developing countries, the prevalence of cash in consumer payment transactions was higher only in Indonesia. In Brazil, by contrast, the figures were 85 per cent and 38 per cent, respectively.

Another market research survey cited in academic studies also indicates a very high dependence on cash at the consumer level, but the figures are different: The share of cash by value in total consumer transactions in India declined between 2007 and 2012, but the fall was only from 90.6 per cent to 86.6 per cent between the two years. In volume terms, cash was estimated to account for 98.8 per cent of the total volume of consumer transactions.[2]

If these estimates are valid then they explain why the withdrawal of 86 per cent of the currency in circulation had such a large impact.

GROWTH IN ELECTRONIC PAYMENTS

Digitalisation of financial transactions at all levels and among all economic agents has been one of the initiatives of the GoI and RBI for over a decade now.

The RBI has been overseeing the greater use of electronic payments. The hardware infrastructure and the framework of

[1] The figures are mentioned in PWC (2014), which are drawn from the 2013 study conducted by Mastercard Advisories and the sources for the data there are listed as MasterCard Advisors analysis, 2013 | BIS CPSS, 2011 | McKinsey Global Payments Map, 2008 | World Bank, 2011 without any more information/elaboration. The data must, therefore, be treated with circumspection.

[2] Euromonitor Passport International figures cited in Joseph et al. (2013).

rules and regulations have been enabled for adoption of electronic payments.

As a result, electronic settlement of transactions between businesses has grown rapidly. Individual consumer use of various electronic/digital instruments such as credit/debit cards and funds transfer through NEFT/RTGS has also grown, via Point of Sale (PoS) devices, the desktop and the mobile phone.

Table 8.2 which reproduces a presentation from the RBI's *Annual Report for 2015–16* gives an idea of the growth of electronic payments and settlements over the three years between 2013–14 and 2015–16 by volume and value. In retail transactions, electronic payment now surpasses that of settlement by cheques.

In keeping with the emphasis on electronic payments, the RBI has continued to explore the different ways in which the use of electronic payments can be broadened and deepened.[3]

The government on its part has also been taking steps in this direction. For example:

- From 2015 onwards, the government has been pushing to use the Jan Dhan-Aadhaar-Mobile (JAM) route to make deemed benefit transfers to beneficiaries. This has been a strategy to reduce the use of cash even among the less well-endowed socio-economic groups.
- In early 2016, the Department of Economic Affairs of the Ministry of Finance had laid down guidelines for the 'Promotion of Payments through Cards and Digital Means'.
- In December 2016 (after demonetisation had been announced), the Committee for Digital Payments, which had been earlier constituted by the Ministry of Finance, submitted its report on the 'Medium Term Recommendations to Strengthen the Digital Payment Ecosystem'.

[3] See, for instance, RBI (2016a and 2016b).

TABLE 8.2: Payments Indicators 2013–14 to 2015–16

Item	*Volume (million)*			*Value (Rs billion)*		
	2013–14	*2014–15*	*2015–16*	*2013–14*	*2014–15*	*2015–16*
1	*2*	*3*	*4*	*5*	*6*	*7*
Systemically Important Financial Market infrastructures (SIFMIs)						
1. RTGS	81.1	92.8	98.3	734,252	754,032	824,578
Total Financial Markets Clearing (2+3+4)	2.6	3.0	3.1	621,570	672,456	721,094
2. CBLO	0.2	0.2	0.2	175,262	167,646	178,335
3. Government Securities Clearing	0.9	1.0	1.0	161,848	179,372	183,502
4. Forex Clearing	1.5	1.8	1.9	284,460	325,438	359,257
Total SIFMIs (1 to 4)	83.7	95.7	101.4	1,355,822	1,426,488	1,545,672
Retail Payments						
Total Paper Clearing (5+6+7)	1,257.3	1,195.8	1,096.4	93,316	85,439	81,861
5. CTS	591.4	964.9	958.4	44,691	66,770	69,889
6. MICR Clearing	440.1	22.4	0.0	30,943	1,850	0

(Contd)

Table 8.2 (Contd)

Item	*Volume (million)*			*Value (Rs billion)*		
	2013–14	*2014–15*	*2015–16*	*2013–14*	*2014–15*	*2015–16*
1	2	3	4	5	6	7
7. Non-MICR Clearing	225.9	208.5	138.0	17,682	16,819	11,972
Total Retail Electronic Clearing (8+9+10+11+12)	1,108.3	1,687.4	3,141.6	47,856	65,366	91,408
8. ECS DR	192.9	226.0	224.8	1,268	1,740	1,652
9. ECS CR	152.5	115.3	39.0	2,492	2,019	1,059
10. NEFT	661.0	927.6	1,252.9	43,786	59,804	83,273
11. Immediate Payment Service (IMPS)	15.4	78.4	220.8	96	582	1,622
12. National Automated Clearing House (NACH)	86.5	340.2	1,404.1	215	1,221	3,802
Total Card Payments (13+14+15)	1,261.8	1,737.7	2,707.2	2,575	3,325	4,484
13. Credit Cards	509.1	615.1	785.7	1,540	1,899	2,407
14. Debit Cards	619.1	808.1	1,173.5	955	1,213	1,589

(Contd)

Table 8.2 (Contd)

Item	*Volume (million)*			*Value (Rs billion)*		
	2013–14	*2014–15*	*2015–16*	*2013–14*	*2014–15*	*2015–16*
1	2	3	4	5	6	7
15. Prepaid Payment Instruments (PPIs)	133.6	314.5	748.0	81	212	488
Total Retail Payments (5 to 15)	3,627.4	4,620.9	6,945.2	143,748	154,129	177,752
Grand Total (1 to 15)	3,711.1	4,716.6	7,046.6	1,499,570	1,580,617	1,723,425

Notes:
1. Real time gross settlement (RTGS) system includes customer and inter-bank transactions only.
2. Settlement of collateralised borrowing and lending obligation (CBLO), government securities clearing and forex transactions are through the Clearing Corporation of India Ltd. (CCIL).
3. Consequent to total cheque volume migrating to the cheque truncation system (CTS), there is no magnetic ink character recognition (MICR) cheque processing centre (CPC) location in the country as of now.
4. The figures for cards are for transactions at point of sale (PoS) terminals only.
5. The National Automated Clearing House (NACH) system was started by the National Payments Corporation of India (NPCI) on December 29, 2012, to facilitate inter-bank, high volume, electronic transactions which are repetitive and periodic in nature.
6. ECS: Electronic clearing service; DR: Debit; CR: Credit; NEFT: National electronic funds transfer.
7. Figures in the columns might not add up to the total due to rounding off.

Source: 'Table IX.1: Payment System Indicators—Annual Turnover', *RBI Annual Report (2015–16)*, page 95 reproduced here.

PACE OF ADOPTION OF DIGITAL PRACTICES

While the economy has been moving towards the greater use of digital transactions, accelerating the pace, especially among individuals and micro-enterprises, calls for a consideration of a number of issues.

The feasibility or what needs to be done to make the shift, needs to grapple with issues relating to infrastructure and consumer preferences:[4]

Infrastructure

The issues to be addressed in infrastructure are many:

Banking Infrastructure

(i) Universal Coverage of Banking/Financial Inclusion

A drive to bring about a much greater spread and depth of digital transactions and much less use of cash would require in the first instance far greater access to banking services among the poor than at present.[5]

---

[4] The issues here are based on the material and arguments contained in RBI (2015), Pahwa (2016) and Nandan Nilekani in TiE (2015) and NDTV (2016).

[5] A 2015 World Bank report placed the adult population in India with a bank account at 53 per cent and the adult female population with a bank account at 43 per cent. This was before the Jan Dhan drive, so the numbers may now be different. A 2015 RBI committee placed the proportion of women with a bank account to just 536 per 1,000 women. There is also a variation in its spread. There is not only a rural–urban inequality in financial inclusion (men and women), but there is also a regional inequality, with the eastern, north-eastern and central states having a much poorer banking coverage.

In the recent years, there has been a significant increase in the number of branches and also in the number of households with savings bank accounts. The growth of the 'no frills' accounts and then more recently of the Jan Dhan accounts has led to an improvement in the extent of financial inclusion. As of 7 December 2016, there were 25.82 crore Jan Dhan accounts with a balance of Rs 74,609 crores. Of these accounts, 23 per cent were zero balance accounts.

(ii) Route to Universal Banking

The thinking now is to use the spread of the mobile phone to achieve near universal banking.

In 2015, an RBI committee recommended that the last mile be covered digitally with mobile phone technology in order to achieve universal or near universal financial inclusion

The presence of 'one billion savings accounts, one billion phones and one billion Aadhaar numbers' is seen as affording an opportunity to traverse the last mile to achieve universal financial inclusion through the mobile phone. In the first instance, Aadhaar can be used to open a bank account with its e-KYC facility. Then, the mobile phone can be used to communicate with the bank and Aadhaar will authenticate the transaction.

The mobile phone can be used to carry out a range of financial services, and not just for making mobile payments. If there is inter-operability, then mobile payments can be made across e-wallets, bank accounts and with merchants.

Technology Infrastructure

(i) Mobile Phone Connection Coverage

For the mobile phone to leap frog credit/debit card use in digital transactions, there will have to be universal mobile connection coverage.

India had 1,034 million mobile phone connection at the end of July 2016. This was a high tele-density of 83 per cent, but included individuals with more than one connection. There was also a regional inequality with the tele-density under 75 per cent in five populous states: Uttar Pradesh (66 per cent), Bihar (55 per cent), Assam (60 per cent), Madhya Pradesh (61 per cent) and Odisha (71 per cent).

A substantial increase in tele-density across the country, especially so in certain large and poor states (where financial inclusion is now low), will be required to enable the use of the mobile phone for executing and authenticating financial transactions.

(ii) Solutions for Segments

Smart phones are the most suitable for digital transactions by individuals. However, there are only about 200–300 million smart phones in the country (2016). Separate solutions need to be offered for: (a) holders of smart phones, (b) holders of feature phones (400–500 million) and (c) those without phone connections.

The National Payments Corporation of India (NPCI) and other agencies have been working on solutions for each population segment. The Unified Payment Interface (UPI) works for smart phones; the Unstructured Supplementary Service Data (USSD) service for those with only feature phones; and microATMs will be available for those without telephones but with accounts through banking correspondents.

These solutions have either just been introduced or are yet to be operationalised. Hence, a shift towards digitalisation with this approach will have to cope with the uncertainties that come with a manifold expansion of new services/solutions.

(iii) Internet Connections

Carrying out digital financial transactions requires Internet connections with large bandwidth. Of the billion plus mobile connections, 322 million or a third are connected to the Internet (March 2016), and of the total Internet connections (wireless and wireline), 44 per cent were broadband connections.

(iv) Reliability

Authentication of a digital connection requires a reliable broadband connection. Outside of the cities and large towns, reliability remains a problem and there are reports of failures in authentication of Aadhaar.

(v) Credit/Debit Cards

As of August 2016, there were an outstanding 26.4 million credit cards and as many as 712.5 million debit cards (it is widely believed that the latter, which includes cards issued to Jan Dhan account holders, does not reflect the number of cards in regular use). The usage of credit card is largely limited to the top 5–10 per cent of the population.

(vi) PoS terminals and microATMs

As of August 2016, India had 1.46 million PoS terminals, which is said to be one of the lowest among the larger developing countries. This would be a very small fraction of the 50–60 million retail enterprises (guess-estimates) in the country. An overwhelming majority of the PoS terminals are located in the urban centres.

An accelerated shift to digital will, therefore, call for a sudden and multiple increase in PoS terminals.

Consumer Preferences

The infrastructure for digitalisation is important, but so too is the ability of the consumer to use electronic payment means. Here there are three sets of relevant issues.

(i) Digital Literacy

Digital transactions call for a minimum awareness of technology, a set of skills and care in executing online transactions. This would, therefore, require government-organised financial and digital 'literacy' programmes on a massive scale that are executed not to 'teach' the citizen, but spread awareness out of concern for her economic security.

The consumers need to be able to read, understand and carry out transactions on the phone/PoS. These are challenges in a society where basic literacy is still 75 per cent.

(ii) Language compatibility

Financial applications are still almost entirely in English. So there will need to be a sea-change in the display of applications for a large proportion of the literate who cannot read english.

(iii) Investment and operating costs

The price of phones has fallen dramatically and while smartphones remain relatively expensive they too are expected to fall in price. Still, for a segment of the population these investment costs will remain barriers to execution of digital transactions. Further, the small operating costs and, in some cases, the hidden costs of conducting digital transactions also add up when compared to cash usage which, for the consumer, is of zero cost.

Privacy and Security

Users of digital instruments for financial transactions must be assured not only of security, but also of privacy, that the large volume of data on their spending practices and financial transactions will not be made available to private parties or to state agencies. As of now, the GoI's view is that privacy is not a fundamental right, in other worlds confidentiality of digital transactions cannot be ensured. As digitalisation expands, users of digital instruments for transactions will look for assurance of privacy if they are to embrace digitalisation.

SUMMING-UP

Digitalisation of financial transactions in the Indian economy had begun well before Demonetisation 2016. In the organised or formal sector, the level of digitalisation is already at a very high level, with electronic payments surpassing settlement by paper cheques.

It is in the informal sector and at the level of individuals that digitalisation has been constrained by a number of factors, including infrastructural issues, unfamiliarity and unaffordability.

While the informal sector does consist of enterprises (in industry and services), which remain 'informal' because they wish to operate outside the pale of the tax authorities and these enterprises depend heavily on cash, the informal sector also consists of a much larger number of self-employed, family and micro-enterprises, which are informal because they are of low productivity. These enterprises fall well below the tax threshold. It is the latter group which for reasons of unfamiliarity and unaffordability will find it more difficult to take to digital instruments, and for whom cash for now remains the most convenient and trusted form of transaction.

Behavioural changes can be encouraged and digitalisation may then well pick up momentum. Behavioural changes cannot, however, be forced; the process of digitalisation also needs to be inclusive.

The government will understandably be interested in making the 'tax avoiding' informal sector adopt digital systems of payment and settlement. The introduction of the Good and Services Tax (GST) should go some way in simultaneously persuading these enterprises to switch to greater use of digital instruments of payment and bring them into the tax net.

In the first couple of months after demonetisation was announced, there was an increase in transactions conducted through a variety of digital means, most notably through mobile wallets. Those who had access to digital platforms could use them for executing transactions. There was at the same time a large proportion of the population, which did not have access to any digital platforms and had to manage with the limited cash in circulation.

The scarcity of cash following demonetisation pushed up the adoption of digital payments to a new level. One will have to wait and see if this will be sustained after cash returns to the system.

Government initiatives seek to push digitalisation further. However, given the many issues that need to be addressed in digitalisation, it will be difficult to vastly accelerate the pace of adoption of electronic means of payment. Cash, with all its advantages for the individual, will remain an important means of transaction.

Section III

— *nine* —

Distress and Despair

The demonetisation of 2016 was not the first of its kind in India's history. But in scale and sweep, it was the biggest ever, and had an impact which extended far beyond the intended targets.

In the two months after demonetisation, all forms of the media reported on the many different impacts it had on people's lives, cutting across all sectors in all parts of the country. Research agencies, academics and field observers also collected primary information on the impact of demonetisation. By mid-January 2017, at least one state government (Kerala) had already made an official assessment of the initial impact of demonetisation.

The immediate experience has, therefore, been richly documented and can be drawn on to get an idea of what happened in the economy and how people were affected.

This chapter is based on media reports and field studies that were published/prepared until mid-January 2017, that is, during the first 10 weeks after the announcement on 8 November.

Macro Impact

Over 85 per cent of India's workers are engaged in the low productivity informal sector in agriculture, industry and services which contributes to 45 per cent of the GDP.[1] The use of cash

---

[1] There is no official definition of the informal sector which is also described as 'unorganised'. The most comprehensive definition is that

is the norm rather than the exception in the informal sector. It is, therefore, to be expected that demonetisation of 86 per cent of the currency in circulation which is not accompanied by a simultaneous or near-simultaneous injection of new currency would disrupt economic activity, leading to a loss of output. And that employment, incomes and consumption would, therefore, decline among the affected groups. The longer the lag between demonetisation and the introduction of fresh currency, the greater is the disruption and loss of output and incomes.

Many private agencies and multilateral institutions have forecast a loss of output which would bring down GDP growth in the fiscal year 2016–17. Table 9.1 presents a compilation of some of the estimates made until mid-January 2017, and gives an idea of the extent of disruption caused by demonetisation. These include the estimates made by the RBI and the Central Statistics Office (CSO). The CSO's advance estimate made in mid-January 2017 did not cover the period after demonetisation.

---

offered by the National Commission for Employment in the Unorganised Sector (NCEUS). The informal sector as defined includes agriculture which, other than of large plantations in the commodity sector, is entirely informal in its organisation. The numbers on the size of the informal sector and the workers in the sector are what detailed studies conducted by the NCEUS came up with using National Sample Survey (NSSO) data, estimates informally updated by Ravi Srivastava, a former member of the NCEUS (e-mail communication).

TABLE 9.1: Forecasts of GDP Growth for 2016–17

(before and after demonetisation, in per cent)

Institution Making Forecast	*Pre 8 November 2016 Estimate of GDP Growth*	*Post 8 November 2016 Estimate of GDP Growth*
1. Ambit Capital (18 November 2016)		
—Fiscal Year (FY) 2016–17	6.8%	3.5%
—FY2017–18	7.3%	5.8%
—3Quarter FY17 (nominal)	11.5%	1.6%
—3Quarter FY17 (deflated)	—	–2.4%
(21 December)		
—FY2016–17	3.5%	3.5%
—FY2017–18	5.8%	5.8%
—1stHalf FY17		6.4%
—2nd Half FY17		0.5%
2. Credit Suisse (16 December 2016)		
—FY2016–17	7.8%	6.9%
3. Reserve Bank of India (7 December 2016)		
Gross Value Added (GVA) growth in second half of FY (H2)	7.7%	
GVA growth in 2016–17	7.6%	7.1
4. Central Statistical Office (Government of India) (6 January 2017)		
GDP growth (2016–17)	7.6%	7.1%
5. Asian Development Bank (13 December 2016)		
GDP growth (2016–17)	7.4%	7%

(Contd)

Table 9.1 (Contd)

Institution Making Forecast	*Pre 8 November 2016 Estimate of GDP Growth*	*Post 8 November 2016 Estimate of GDP Growth*
6. Fitch Ratings (10 January 2017)		
GDP growth (2016–17)	7.4%	6.9%
7. Morgan Stanley		
GDP growth (2016–17)	7.6%	7.3%
8. Care Ratings (18 November 2016)		
GDP growth (2016–17)	7.8%	7.5%–7.3%
GVA growth (2016–17)	7.6%	7.1%
9. ICRA Ratings		
GDP growth (2016–17)	7.9%	7.5%
GVA growth (2016–17)	—	6.6% (lower than before)
10. World Bank Economic Prospects (January 2017)		
GDP growth (2016–17)	7.6%	7%
11. International Monetary Fund (16 January 2017)		
GDP growth (2016–17)	7.6%	6.6%
GDP growth (2017–18)	7.6%	7.2%
12. Centre for Monitoring the Indian Economy, Economic Outlook (12 January 2017)		
GDP growth (2016–17)	7.6% (approx)	6%
GDP growth five years till 2020–21	7.6% to 8.5%	Under 7%

Notes: 1. Figures in brackets in column 1 are dates when forecasts were made/ published.
2. Sources are listed along with the bibliography for the chapter.

An Overview

The huge cash crunch in the two months after November 2016 has had its inevitable impact. There has been an economic slowdown, in some vulnerable sectors output has even contracted. With the slowing down has come a slower growth of incomes, and again in some cases an actual loss in income. This must have affected consumption as well, especially among those of a lower socio-economic status who are more vulnerable to dips in the economy. Going by all reports, it is among the daily workers, the women, self-employed, and the elderly without security who have suffered the most in terms of loss of employment and income. There has also been hardship because of the inability/delay in obtaining cash for daily consumption.

It would appear that the downturn was the combined result of the shortage of liquidity, and the income effect of demonetisation. The reports did not indicate any major wealth effect of demonetisation.

Some leading economists who have criticised demonetisation have also said that it has caused unnecessary hardship and that it has hurt the middle, lower-middle and poor classes, and that pain has been inflicted on those who were not the intended targets. Others have even described demonetisation as 'an assault on the poor'.

From the media reports that have been published, it would seem that the hardship that the disruption caused was widespread but unequally distributed. It was more in rural than in urban India. In urban India, the impact was felt more in the informal sector of industry and services. There appears to be a regional pattern as well. In agriculture, the north and east seem to have been affected the most and the south the least, with the west falling in between. The media confirmed that the hardship was experienced most by those least capable of coping with the fallout of the cash crunch: the casual and daily wage workers who did not enjoy social protection of any kind.

It would be useful to describe and discuss the nature of the impact of demonetisation in each sector. It would also be instructive to learn about the adjustment mechanisms that people strived to put in place in order to cope.[2]

AGRICULTURE

Agriculture depends heavily on cash for its operations. The shortage of cash affected marketing of the kharif (monsoon) crop and sowing of the rabi (winter) crop, with the more visible impact being felt in market arrivals and prices for farmers. The fallout was also more where perishable commodities were produced.

Unfortunately, the disruption came at a time when agriculture was recovering from the drought in the previous year. The impact was felt down the line from traders who saw business fall to farmers who received lower prices and most of all among labourers who received delayed wage payments and then experienced a decline in employment.

Marketing

> *An eerie calm welcomes you at the 'galla' (grain)* mandi *in Bhind town [Madhya Pradesh]. The sprawling grain shed where farmers offload their produce is uncharacteristically clean, and absolutely empty. Around 90% of the wholesale grain shops that flank the market remain shuttered. Except for a lone truck being loaded at the far end, there's no sign of activity.*

[2] The bibliography to this chapter gives all the references to the illustrations cited here. It is also a larger list referring to some of the special issues/series on the impact of demonetisation published in the media.

The mandi normally handles around 1,000 bags of grain per day during this season, says Devendra Jain, [a] ... trader. "But this time, we have been getting just 50 to 100 bags," he says.

—*The Times of India*, 10 January 2010

Produce markets were immediately disrupted after 8 November 2016 as farmers found it difficult to market what they had just harvested. Most mandis worked on a cash basis and since the commission agents did not have cash, farmers could not sell their produce—unless they did so on credit. It was not until late November and early December that some mandis in some states hurried to introduce cheque/electronic payments. The impact of that was limited since to function smoothly all parties needed to have bank accounts, or at least some of them should have been able to withdraw cash above the ceilings.

There were regional differences, with the south where the kharif harvest had been marketed before demonetisation being less affected than the north where the harvest came in after 8 November 2016. The situation varied from crop to crop and, of course, also depended on whether the mandis (markets) were more or less dependent on cash.

The overall impact was that in some commodities (cereals, pulses and oilseeds), market arrivals were vastly lower than normal. In the perishable commodities, initially it was the prices which crashed rather than market arrivals, since farmers had no choice but to bring the produce to the market.

Market arrivals plummeted in the first month after demonetisation. Researchers collected information showing a decline of more than 50 per cent in some crops in the first week after demonetisation. Occasionally, farmers were even compelled to accept payments in the demonetised notes. Over time, some mandis made arrangements for payments by cheque. But reports continued into January 2017 of mandis being deserted and farmers being unable to market their produce because traders did not have adequate cash with them.

The difficulties experienced by producers of perishable commodities like fruits and vegetables, were different and in some respects more acute. In the absence of additional cold storage facilities to handle the emergency, producers had to bring the produce to the market. However, in the absence of buyers, prices collapsed, in some cases by much more than for cereals, pulses and oilseeds. There were also isolated reports from the south that farmers in some cases had no choice, but to abandon the produce on the roads.

The important fishery producing states of Kerala, Goa, Tamil Nadu, Andhra Pradesh and Maharashtra reported similar problems. Prices crashed in the first month after demonetisation in wholesale and retail markets as the cash crunch kept buyers away. This had a chain impact on owners of boats and fish workers as fishing activity reduced. Activities picked up again in December 2016, but even in January 2017 there were reports of less than normal fishing activity off the east and west coasts. The combined effect was an impact on the diets in states such as Bengal and Kerala where fish is an important constituent of the daily intake of food.

Sowing

> *Ram Gati Kushwaha, from Langra [Etawah District, UP]: ... "I am a farmer with just three* bighas *of land and I am struggling. I have no money to sow for the next season. Though I can borrow money for seeds, how will I get fertiliser and pay the labourers? It is impossible".*
>
> —*The Indian Express*, 8 December 2016

The media reported that after the difficulties with the marketing of the kharif crop, a fresh round of difficulties emerged with sowing of the rabi crop. The government permitted purchase of seed with the demonetised notes from government outlets. However, there were other inputs like fertilisers to be purchased and labourers to be hired and paid. Since traders of inputs function on cash and credit basis, reporters spoke of farmers increasing their credit lines because of the cash crisis.

Field observers also wrote of an increase in debt to non-bank sources because of the cash crunch. The overall scarcity of cash meant that even if the farmers had managed to sell their kharif crop, they would either be paid in instalments (cash) or would not be able to withdraw adequate amounts of money from banks. They, therefore, had to borrow from private money-lenders (where possible). Observers also spoke of those who had received poor prices for their kharif crop having to bear the double burden of not being able to service the existing loans and then being forced to borrow for the rabi sowing season.

Contrary to initial fears, official statistics reported a growth in rabi sowing over the drought-affected base of 2015. Commentators, however, pointed out that the government data also reported a slowing down of the pace of growth with the passing of each week after demonetisation, reflecting perhaps the underlying difficulties.

The full impact of cash withdrawal on rabi sowing and output would be known only when the rabi crop is harvested in March–April 2017. In early January, officials of NITI Aayog came to the tentative conclusion that demonetisation had only a minor impact on output and farm incomes.

Independent analysts of the rural scene, however, concluded after field visits that there had been a visible impact on agriculture which had affected non-agricultural activities as well. They reported, more worryingly, that no immediate recovery could be expected.

RURAL LABOUR

> *Bhatta (brick kiln) workers ... said that because of (the) cash shortage, bhatta owners told them not to come. "I used to work at a Bhatta nearby earning about Rs 250 daily. But it has not opened since Diwali (October 2016). Before that it was closed for the rains. So, actually I am unemployed for five months", said Ashish Kumar, a Dalit resident of Ankodiya village in Etawah.*
>
> —*The Times of India*, 11 January 2017

> *"Bade aadmi ko kya. Mar to gareeb raha hai (It's the poor who get crushed)", says Abdul Aigaz, a shoe factory worker who left his first job after the owner failed to pay him. He soon found another but the owner paid him Rs 1,500, in three old Rs 500 denomination notes, and sent him home. "My son has his exams coming up, he is asking for a guide book, and all I can think of is how I can feed him", he says.*
>
> —*The Indian Express*, 25 December 2016

Observers in rural India pointed to the impact on those least able to cope—the rural casual labourers. These labourers were affected in different ways. One, the casual labourer in agriculture is usually paid weekly or even daily in cash. Cash scarcity meant that payments by the employer were delayed. In some cases, unfortunately, their employers even paid them with demonetised currency. Two, where rabi sowing operations were delayed or even declined, work and then wage payments were affected. The result was a reported increase in personal debt where local retail traders were willing to extend credit to the labourers. Three, where agriculture was affected, non-agricultural activities were also affected. There was a decline in employment and, therefore, income. As a result, the labourers were even driven to desperate measures.[3]

---

[3] 'Out of cash and desperate, 35-year-old Puran Sharma from Aligarh got himself sterilised ... for the Rs 2,000 a man gets for the procedure.... "I am in dire need of money to keep the house hearth burning. Besides

The fallout of the hardship experienced by rural labourers was that there was a 60 per cent increase in the demand for work under the National Rural Employment Guarantee Act (NREGA) in December 2016, an increase in demand that extended to the first week of January 2017.[4]

ADJUSTMENT MECHANISMS: THE NEW AND BREAKDOWN OF THE OLD

Starved of cash, 15 farmers of a village in Gwalior deposited 45 quintals of paddy as their children's school fees.

—*The Times of India*, 25 December 2016

The cash crunch due to demonetisation did force workers to leave their jobs and go back home.... The primary reason why the textile hub of Tirupur suffered is because of the migration of the labour force. We cannot blame workers who came from different parts of India including Uttar Pradesh and Bihar as we could not provide them wages.

—G. R. Senthilvel, owner of a textile firm in Tirupur, Tamil Nadu, *Mint*, 27 January 2017

In the first month after demonetisation, there were reports of unusual forms of transactions as the residents of rural India tried to cope with the shortage of cash.

Transactions that represented a different kind of demonetisation were reported: payment in kind became a form of exchange. Farmers paid traders in part or full in grain, so too payment to

---

I do not know anybody in the cash-dry village who has enough money to lend me some. The local ASHA didi told me about it and we decided to go for it'" (Jaiswal and Chauhan 2016). 'In times of notebandi, nasbandi rises', *The Times of India*, 27 November 2016.

[4] There is, however, some dispute about whether the spike in work demand in December 2016 was unusual and, therefore, could be linked to an outcome of employment loss after demonetisation.

farm labourers. Such practices were to be found more in the rural hinterland, away from the cities, where the cash crunch was the most severe.

Barter practices were also noticed in the initial weeks in north-east India where again the shortage of cash was initially felt more than elsewhere.

In the post-demonetisation scenario, the situation also compelled labourers to accept some unfortunate terms. A number of media reports mentioned that farmers were continuing to pay labourers in the demonetised currency. The workers then had to travel to the nearest bank and stand in lines to exchange the notes or have them exchanged at a discount through commission agents.

The biggest adjustment mechanism forced on rural India was the return of a large number of migrants. Across the country, the freezing of commerce and the shutdown of many small and medium enterprises in the informal sector in the cities and towns, led to migrant workers returning to their villages. The migrants returned when they were not paid their wages over extended periods, or because their employers had to shut shop (see further).

Migration which had been an adjustment mechanism for residents of very poor areas like Bundelkhand in Uttar Pradesh had broken down. The situation was now reversed. The villages had to provide economic and social security to the migrants who had returned. The return put additional pressure on rural society.

INDUSTRY

> *We had a monthly turnover of Rs 3 crore before November 8, now it has reduced to half. Consequently, we had to cut jobs by more than 50 per cent.... We supply components to Hero Motocorp and with a reduction in demand for two-wheelers the ancillary units like ours are bound to*

suffer. The situation is no different for several hundred ancillary units in the automobile sector in this region.

—Karn Talwar, owner of an ancillary unit in Gurgaon, Haryana, *The Hindu*, New Delhi, 13 January 2017

Owner Jamshed Soleja [of a slaughter house-cum-tanning unit in Unnao, Uttar Pradesh] is putting in place lay-off plans. He claims that the unit has closed due to lack of cash....“We have been shut since December 1 and have communicated this to our 1,200 employees. While we can pay for our supplies through cheques, we require cash for the auction of animals in local markets and for the labourers. With supply getting affected, there was no point holding them back.” Soleja adds that he has had to cancel his overseas orders. “I have returned 20 per cent advance payment from companies in China.”

—*The Indian Express*, 25 December 2016

The organised sections of Indian industry initially did not seem to be affected very much by demonetisation. The first round of official statistics after demonetisation even showed a pick-up in the manufacturing growth rate.

The media, industry organisations and researchers, however, found that the micro, small and medium enterprises (MSME), and the larger informal sector were deeply affected. Later, when the financial results for the corporate sector for the third quarter (October–December) of the financial year 2016–17 began to be published, it became apparent that the organised sector too had experienced a slowdown.[5]

---

[5] The initial batch of results for the third quarter of 2016–17 (October–December) of companies in the consumer goods segments when released in the first fortnight of January did show a worsening of financial indicators, suggesting that demonetisation had had an impact on the organised segment as well. The larger impact was experienced by companies serving the rural markets (for example, tractors) or producing goods for consumers outside the higher income brackets (for example,

One industry organisation, the All-India Manufacturers' Organisation concluded in early January, based on a study among its members, that in the first 34 days after demonetisation its members from the micro and small-scale segment saw a 50 per cent drop in revenue and shed 35 per cent of their workforce. The situation was expected to worsen by March 2017. An industry association would be expected to speak on behalf of its members; independent agencies also reported a steep loss in businesses in the MSME sector.

Reporters who fanned out across the country found much the same story. One investigation in mid-December of small units in Dharavi, Mumbai (leather), Bhiwandi, Maharashtra (textiles), Sivakasi, Tamil Nadu (crackers) and Solapur, Maharashtra (beedis) showed a common pattern: the operation of twin pressures. A shortage of cash squeezed operations and a decline in demand affected sales.

The situation was not very different in small-scale enterprises producing for the export market. Newspapers reported that in Tirupur, the export textile centre in Tamil Nadu, the larger enterprises were not affected, but even six weeks after demonetisation, in mid-December 2016, some of the smaller ones remained affected by a scarcity of cash. Export transactions in these units were conducted electronically, but workers were paid in cash. Workers reported delays in wage payments by more than a fortnight and when delayed further they chose to leave.

Payment of wages in cash, especially to contract labour, was the norm in small, medium and even large companies. Going digital or even opening bank accounts was not a simple job for workers even in cities. In the NOIDA region of Uttar Pradesh, centre

---

motorcycles). Companies in the fast moving consumer goods industry, however, also reported poor results in the third quarter (*Business Standard* 2017).

of many large garment export units, wage payment to contract labour (the main constituent of the labour force) had been all in cash. One media report said that workers, most of them migrant workers, found it difficult to open bank accounts on their own and employers had refused to help, fearing subsequent demands for them to be made permanent. The employing firms, unable to pay cash wages, laid off hundreds of workers by December 2016. In the NOIDA region, up to 40 per cent of contract workers were reported to have been laid off.

Overall, the decline in business was expected to reverse itself as more and more cash got injected into the system and as small companies too turned digital for receipts and payments. There were some reports on those lines. But there were also reports of a continuing sluggishness in demand. For instance, in January 2017, at one of India's largest manufacturers of motorcycles and scooters, contract workers who had been laid off in end-November 2016 had not yet been taken back. The human impact of such lay-offs was agonising,

> Vikas Sahu, 30, who had been working at Hero for four years, has been unable to send money back to his parents, wife and children, who live in his village about 100 miles west of New Delhi. His first grader's school fees are overdue by months, and his father took out a loan of 70,000 rupees ... for agricultural expenses, including paying for repairs on the family's tractor. "How long I can survive like this?" he asked.
>
> —*New York Times*, 24 January 2017

RETAIL TRADE

Companies in the organised sector cut back on production because of a lack of demand and so did small enterprises because of a lack of working capital in cash. It was to be expected then that retail trade too would report a fall in sales.

This indeed was so. Media surveys of wholesale and retail markets in cities and towns reported a lower volume of sales by upwards of 30 per cent in the first two months after demonetisation. Large and small retail enterprises were affected, the smaller ones because they did not have access to cash and nor did their customers.

Retail trade on pavements and in small shops is an important source of livelihood and even a survival strategy for families at the lower end of the socio-economic scale in the towns and cities. The impact of the aftermath of Demonetisation 2016 was, according to reports, particularly hard on them.

Surveys of the impact on petty trade did show a steep fall in business. Table 9.2 presents the results of one such survey by a team of academics of 85 small traders/service establishments in Ranchi a month after demonetisation.

TABLE 9.2: Post-Demonetisation Decline in Economic Activity

(85 shops/vendors/traders in Ranchi)

Nature of business	*Self-reported decline in earnings (%)*
Labour contractors (2), fruit seller, tailor	81–100
Chicken shops (2), gift corner, tent house, welding shop, hardware, mobile shop, utensils, crockery shop, garments shop, shoe shop, electrical appliances, flower seller, cobbler	61–80
Garments shop (3), tailors (2), carpenters (2), welding shops (2), mobile shops (2), hardware (2), cycle-rickshaw puller (2), grocery shops (2), mutton shops (2), fruit sellers (3), dry fruits, sugarcane juice, eggrolls, watch shop, electrical appliances, fish shop, crockery shop, garage, stationary, labour contractor	41–60

(Contd)

Table 9.2 (Contd)

Nature of business	*Self-reported decline in earnings (%)*
Bicycles shops (2), garments shops (2), pan shop, snacks seller, golgappa, pan gumti, grocery shop, watch shop, optician, stationary, eggrolls, fruitseller, mobile shop, hardware, garage,	21–40
Crockery shops (2), shoe shop, fruitseller, dhaba, stationary, cobbler, garage	1–20
Newspaper hawker, autowalla, bookshop, chicken shop, hardware, barber, cosmetics, khainee[b], private vehicle transport[b]	0

Notes: [a] Numbers in brackets indicate cases of multiple observations.
[b] Minor *increase* in earnings.

Source: 'Demonetisation Decimates Ranchi's Economy', Jean Dreze, Dheeraj Kumar and Akash Ranjan, 26 December 2016, available at https://thewire.in/89498/demonetisation-decimates-ranchis-economy/, accessed on 30 December 2016.

IMPACT ON WOMEN

> *My husband doesn't know about the little savings I have earned working in the fields. He would beat me if I disclose it to him. My neighbours and other women have promised to get me new notes.*
>
> —Hosna Bibi in Madargi village, Bidar District, Karnataka, *Quint*, 5 January 2017

Women in female-headed households, women in low wage employment and women in low productivity self-employment were at particular risk after demonetisation. Much of this work used and was paid for in cash. The drying up of working capital made it difficult for women to earn this meagre and yet important income. The economic slowdown added to the threat to this income, which was usually their only independent source of income.

One of the little-known survival strategies that many poor Indian women follow came to light in the media when Demonetisation 2016 tragically imperilled the fruits of these strategies.

Women in male-headed households who are effectively safeguarding the interests of the family have been known to put away savings bit by bit over the years for use in an emergency or for the children. These savings are kept almost entirely in cash and hidden from the male head of the household. They are not kept in a bank account either because the woman does not have one or she is worried that if she does have one it will be discovered and emptied by the husband/father/brother.

Media reports brought out cases where the need to exchange these notes in the old series for new ones put at risk these valuable savings and even the physical well-being of the women.

Other fall-back strategies for women were also affected after demonetisation. Self-help groups, which usually comprise mainly women, functioned on receipt of small loans and repayments in cash. Post-demonetisation, most micro-finance institutions reported a decline in disbursals.

Waiting in Lines

Haroon's son Muneer died on November 19, after he had carried the nine-year-old for more than 30 km through the forests seeking medical attention. Precious time was lost as Haroon [a nomad in Samba district of Jammu and Kashmir] couldn't exchange the Rs 29,000 he had at the time for new currency...Haroon says that's what he can't live with—that he had the means to save Muneer but couldn't.

—*The Indian Express*, 8 January 2017

Humko apna paisa kyon nahi dete. Pehle tayyari kyon nahi ki.... (*Why aren't they giving me my money? Why didn't they prepare*), *Lal said, echoing sentiments of millions of people standing in queues for hours outside banks and ATMs across the country. [78-year-old Nand Lal who burst into tears at Gurgaon after waiting for three days to withdraw part of his army pension.]*

—*Hindustan Times*, 16 December 2016

One of the first set of reports that recounted the agony of people coping with demonetisation were those about people at hospitals running from pillar to post because the hospitals would not receive advance payments in old notes. These were families with neither insurance nor credit cards and they, therefore, had to make payment in cash.

There were reports in the initial days of patients being turned away, and some then even dying because the money their families possessed had turned worthless and the hospitals would not admit the patients. These were tragedies as much inflicted by heartless hospital managements as by the sudden withdrawal of legal tender to currency people had lawfully earned.

The lasting public memory of Demonetisation 2016 will be of the long and quiet queues of people waiting at banks to deposit their stock of demonetised currency and then to withdraw the amounts permitted by the (changing) regulations.

The time lag between the withdrawal of currency and the infusion of new currency meant that there was for many weeks a very limited distribution of cash to the banks. The ATMs first had to be calibrated to handle the new series of notes; later banks preferred to distribute the cash at their branches rather than stock the ATMs. So the lines were concentrated at the branches of banks.

Men and women, young and old, had to spend long hours—in some cases come back day after day—to withdraw a limited amount of cash. They had to do this for weeks together since the weekly cash withdrawal ceilings until mid-January 2017 were very low.

Daily wage workers spoke of having to forego a day's wages because they had to stand in a line for hours to withdraw money from the bank. Pensioners spoke of delays in remittances and having to make repeated visits. For any working person, it was time that had to be diverted from work to stand in queue, not once but many times over in November and December 2016.

The queues in all parts of the country continued into December 2016 and even into early January 2017. Newspapers spoke of dozens of people—some reports said more than a 100—dying while standing in queue, and commentators jousted about whether they died because of demonetisation or due to natural causes.

Whatever the long-term cause of the deaths, the tragedy was that they died standing in line to withdraw what was their money that they had placed in trust in banks.

SUMMING-UP

The numbers on the slowdown in economic growth after Demonetisation 2016 do not capture the hardship that the currency withdrawal of November 2016 inflicted on large sections of the population.

The story of demonetisation and its aftermath, in the first two months after the event, has been one of unremitting pain and hardship inflicted on the people who could not escape its impact. That they may have borne it stoically does not mean that their suffering was any less.

The decision by the government to strip 86 per cent of the currency in circulation of its status as legal tender, followed by the restrictions on withdrawals from banks and then the general shortage of cash, deeply hurt people at different levels and in different dimensions.

Delegalisation of such a large amount of currency—much of which had been used in everyday transactions—shook people's faith in the 'promise to pay the bearer' which is the basic premise of the trust that any currency enjoys. It was no solace to the public when it was then told that it had not lost its money, but could exchange the demonetised currency at banks for new currency notes. The hurdles that people had to overcome to exchange old for new and the limits that were placed on weekly withdrawals made them feel that they were being made to ask for what was not theirs.

The ceilings that lasted for weeks and months on how much savers could draw of the savings that was legitimately theirs strained their faith in the government and the RBI. People were put through physical and psychological strain to access these savings. The physical strain of having to wait in line for hours on end had to initially be repeated every week. The bewilderment of having to go through this process to access their honest savings was no less painful.

The withdrawal of legal tender of such a large amount of currency and then the scarcity of new currency also had painful material impacts which seemed to affect all sections of people in every walk of life—other than, of course, those who had the means and ability to get the better of the system.

Families with sick found that the cash they had was not acceptable at private hospitals. Vegetable vendors found that the cash they used as working capital was temporarily useless. Women who had scrimped and saved for the family and hidden the cash from abusive husbands found their savings were now out in the open; they feared that questions would be asked about their modest savings, and they faced new threats of violence from their husbands. Migrant workers, whose families in villages depended on weekly or monthly remittances, found that they could not send money home. Parents found they could not draw sufficient cash in time from the banks to pay school fees for their children. The elderly found that they had to cope with the same constraints on cash withdrawals as everybody else.

All this pain took on a new and even more difficult form when the self-employed found they had no cash to buy material and no one to buy what they produced. Small enterprises shut down in the city and the village, workers were not paid and then let go. Migrant workers were compelled to return home without work and without savings. Economic activity in many areas which provided work and income to the not-so-fortunate ground to a halt.

At the same time, activities which the wealthy organised and patronised seem not to have been disturbed. Events like lavish weddings in the families of leading politicians were organised as elaborately and as garishly as before with massive expenditure and an enormous display of wealth by the hosts and the invitees.

While the honest citizen found herself without work or waiting in queues at banks to draw small amounts of her savings, the holders of black money were not worried. They were able to find ways, to circumvent demonetisation, launder their black money and deposit it in banks. Faced with this circumvention, the government appeared to lose its professed determination to attack black money. Midway through the demonetisation exercise, it announced an amnesty scheme for holders of black money (the second of 2016), under which those who came forward would be allowed to keep, first, 25 per cent of their black money, and then after four years, they would get back another 25 per cent. So much for the unaccounted cash turning worthless after 8 November 2016.

This in brief has been the impact of Demonetisation 2016 on those on whose behalf the war on black money was unleashed. The wealthy and the criminal as usual did not experience any of this pain. It was those who had the least capacity to cope who bore the entire burden.

— *ten* —

Black Money and Politics*

The Prime Minister in his speech to the nation on 31 December 2016 made a mention of black money and politics:

> Political parties, political leaders and electoral funding, figure prominently in any debate on corruption and black money.
>
> I urge all parties and leaders to move away from a "holier than thou approach", to come together in prioritising transparency, and take firm steps to free politics of black money and corruption.

A reference to politics and black money in the on-going debate about demonetisation is an exception.[1] The political parties which by and large have been critical of demonetisation have been silent about black money in politics. But politics as practised in India is by all accounts an important source of generation and use of black money.

The discourse on politics and black money is often confined to the funding of political parties. However, funding cannot be divorced from the functioning of political parties. In the context of black money and politics, the line between party funds and personal funds of the leadership is often thin. Obviously, it is black

*The proposals in the Union Budget for 2016–17 on electoral funding are discussed in the chapter, 'Demonetisation: An Unfolding Story'.

[1]Another exception is the demand by one of the smaller national parties, the Communist Party of India (CPI), to remove black money from politics.

money that facilitates a blurring of the distinction between what belongs to a party and to the political leaders. Being in public office or in a position to participate in parliamentary debates enhances the scope for generating black money.

Newspapers, TV and the Internet have discussed issues like cash in election spending and options for public funding. But discussions on the larger interface between black money and politics in governance have been scarce.

It is hard to find firm evidence about the use of black money in politics, but instances of the transfer of cash bags to influence voting behaviour in Parliament have been in the public domain. It is generally believed that there has been a two-way bond between electoral politics and black money which has evolved over the years in India. Political activity—during elections in particular—feeds off black money, and, just as important, black money feeds off politics.

FINANCES OF POLITICAL PARTIES

Political parties registered with the Election Commission of India (ECI) enjoy exemption from payment of income and wealth taxes as long as they submit audited accounts of income and expenditure.

Over the years, Supreme Court and high court rulings, and amendments to the Representation of the People's Act 1951 have led to more disclosure than there used to be earlier about party accounts and the finances of candidates in elections. However, the rules on disclosure are such that the political parties can hide more than they reveal about their sources of income.

According to ECI rules, political parties need to record only the details of individual donations of more than Rs 20,000 and communicate these to the Commission. Donations of less than Rs 20,000 are exempt from disclosure requirements and can be accepted in cash.

An overwhelming proportion of the income of political parties is received in the form of individual donations of less than Rs 20,000 each.

The most recent analysis (January 2017) by the NGO, the Association for Democratic Reforms (ADR), which has worked for more than two decades for greater transparency in party finances, has shown that between 2004–05 and 2014–15, 69 per cent of the total declared income of six national parties and 51 recognised regional parties came from donations of less than Rs 20,000 each.[2] In other words, a large majority of the recorded income of the political parties comes from unknown sources.

The dependence on small donations would have been good in itself but for the fact that there is reason to believe that a major part of these collections from 'unknown sources' are actually donations of black money that have been broken up into individual ones of less than Rs 20,000 in cash, solely in order to hide their nature and size.

If some political parties accept black money in cash to finance their political activities, there are organisations which appear to register themselves as 'political parties' in order to launder black money into white.

At the end of 2016, there were seven national recognised parties, 58 state recognised parties and as many as 1,786 unrecognised parties registered with the ECI. In December 2016, the Commission deregistered 255 of these unrecognised political parties for being inactive and for not having contested any elections between 2005 and 2015.

It would appear that a much larger number of registered political parties are not contesting elections, but are enjoying the

[2] Sixteen per cent of income came from declared donors, while another 15 per cent from the sale of assets, membership fees, etc. A similar analysis by Gowda and Sridharan (2012) of the donations received by the Congress and BJP for 2008–09 shows a similar pattern.

tax benefits that come from being registered with the ECI. One analysis of the situation in 2014 noted that of the 1,646 parties registered with the ECI in April 2014, 464 (28 per cent) contested in the 2014 parliamentary elections. That left at the time as many as 1,182 political parties that were dormant but yet availed of the tax benefits that come from enjoying registration with the ECI.

Since the details of all donations received do not have to be declared and since the tax benefits are substantial, it is likely that these 'inactive' political parties are used to launder black money into white.

EXPENDITURE ON ELECTIONS

As long ago as the early 1970s, the Wanchoo Committee on black money noted the entry of black money into the election campaigns.

It is now widely held that black money is an integral part of election spending. It is spent in large amounts and has become one of the mainstays of campaign finance. The greater use of black money is associated with the greater wealth of candidates contesting elections and the rising expenditure on election campaigns.

The ceilings on expenditure that a candidate can spend on her/his election campaign are periodically revised. Since 2014, Lok Sabha candidates can spend up to Rs 70 lakhs and candidates to the state legislative assemblies up to Rs 28 lakhs. This now includes the candidate's own expenditure as well as that by her/his political party.[3]

---

[3] However, certain kinds of expenditure by political parties are by law not included in the election campaign expenditure permissible by the individual candidate. Important exclusions are spending on the party programme and on campaigning by 'star campaigners', which as the title suggests, is of campaigns by important party functionaries. These

An analysis by the ADR of expenditure of 540 Members of Parliament (MPs) elected to the Lok Sabha in 2014 showed that the average expenditure was only Rs 40.40 lakhs or 57 per cent of the ceiling. A third (178 MPs) of the elected MPs reported to have spent less than 50 per cent of the ceiling.

The numbers on actual expenses incurred on individual items during an election campaign show unrealistically low levels. A few examples from the detailed listing in ADR's analysis:

- Of the expenditure filings of 540 MPs in 2014, 166 (31 per cent) MPs declared that they had not received any funds from any person/company/firm/associations/body of persons, etc. as loan, gift or donation
- 109 (20 per cent) MPs declared zero-spending on public meetings, processions, etc. with star campaigners.
- 72 (13 per cent) MPs declared zero-spending on campaign materials.

The reliability of such numbers on expenditure submitted to the ECI is, therefore, in some doubt.

Media reports of the election spending by the winners and the runners-up in Assembly and Lok Sabha elections, however, suggest levels of expenditure well above the ECI ceilings.

In 2013, a Member of the Lok Sabha was widely reported in the media to have said that he had spent Rs 8 crore on his campaign in the 2009 Lok Sabha elections.[4] In 2012, the Chief Election Commissioner (CEC) of the time was reported in the media to have said that a total of Rs 10,000 crore had been spent

---

two items can add up to a considerable amount and can constitute an important exclusion from the ceiling on election expenditure.

[4] See *The Hindu* (2013). The ceiling at the time was Rs 25 lakhs and the MP was later reported to have informed the ECI that he had been only speaking in general terms about the rising cost of elections and the use of black money.

on the Assembly elections in Uttar Pradesh that year.[5] This would be approximately Rs 25 crore of spending by all candidates in each constituency.

Since a very wide gap is observed between what candidates file as their expenses and what is visible as having been spent, it is generally believed that a good proportion of spending on elections is in the form of black money. The main items of expenditure are on pay-outs in kind and cash, transport (hiring, fuel), and organisation of rallies—all of which are believed to be paid largely in cash. There is now greater regulation of spending on campaign material like pamphlets, posters, buntings, etc. The black money spent on unregulated items is much larger.

ASSETS OF CANDIDATES AND LEGISLATORS

The candidates in state and parliamentary elections are getting wealthier, and the proportion of winners is higher among the wealthier candidates (on the latter, see Table 10.1)

TABLE 10.1: Entry Barriers to Political Office: Financial Assets and Chances of Winning

Value of Assets	*No. of Candidates*	*No. of Winners*	*% of Winners*
Very high (Rs 50 million and above	322	106	33
High (Rs 5–50 million)	1,485	283	19
Medium (Rs 1–5 million)	1,785	116	6
Low (less than Rs 1 million)	3,437	15	0.44
Total	7,029	520	7.4

Source: Table 4 reproduced from Gowda and Sridharan (2012: 236) which was based on ADR data for 2009 Lok Sabha elections.

[5] Both these items of news are referenced in Sastry (2014: 37, 41).

Wealthier candidates have a greater chance of winning elections, and the winners are recording a disproportionate increase in the value of their assets when in office.

Since the late 1990s, candidates have had to disclose information about their assets and liabilities (but not income) in affidavits to the ECI. One important piece of ADR-based research which analysed and compared the assets of winning candidates five years later with that of the defeated candidates over the same period arrived at one striking conclusion: The assets of the winners had increased by 222 per cent in the intervening period and that of the non-winners by 134 per cent.[6]

BUSINESS AND POLITICS

Indian business has always been represented in Parliament and the state assemblies. This has been so since the very first elections of 1952.

All anecdotal evidence indicates that the presence of legislators with a business background in both Parliament and the state assemblies has been growing. Systematic analysis of MPs

[6] The analysis compared the assets of the winning candidates who contested again five years later with those of the losing candidates who also contested five years later. The analysis covered the period 2004 to 2013, and examined candidates in all Assembly and Lok Sabha elections during those years. According to the study, 'Of the 3,452 candidates who contested more than one election, 2,967 showed an increase in wealth. This includes all those who contested elections more than once between 2004 and 2013 and includes all state Assembly elections, and the Lok Sabha and Rajya Sabha elections, since all of them went to the polls at least twice during this period. The average declared wealth of such re-contesting candidates in 2004 was Rs 1.74 crore, and Rs 4.08 crore in 2013, an increase of 134 per cent. For winners, the average assets went up from Rs 1.8 crore to Rs 5.81 crore, an increase of 222 per cent. Winners are able to increase their wealth much faster than other candidates' (Sastry 2014: 38).

in successive houses of Parliament also establishes this increasing presence of persons with a business background since the 1990s.[7]

Based on observations in Karnataka, Sridharan and Gowda (2012: 235) write,

> Political party preference for wealthy candidates can give rise to a new breed of "political entrepreneurs" who are ready to invest in running for office in the hope of controlling the levers of government to further enhance their personal wealth.

Sastry (2014: 38) writes,

> In a repeat of the muscle man turned politician of the 1980s, we now see the moneyed-person turned-politician today. A senior leader of one political party once told this writer that 92% of the applications for tickets were from builders and real estate businessmen in one southern city. The leader of the rival party agreed with this.

Historically, business and politics had links even during the freedom movement. But in the recent years, particularly since the reforms of the early 1990s, more leaders of business have taken to politics. More importantly, political leaders have taken to business. The link more often works through the 'close relatives' as defined in the income tax law. The links are not confined to the leadership; the links have had a trickle-down effect to all the layers of government and parties. However, each layer of politics and government has its unique source and use of black money, and the role of cash at each level varies.

---

[7] In an analysis which stops at the 14th Lok Sabha (2004–09), Sinha (2010; Table 30.3) has shown the growing presence of businesspersons in Parliament (both Lok Sabha and Rajya Sabha). Much depends on the classification the researchers use and the self-reporting of the MPs. Still, the analysis shows the 14th Lok Sabha with the highest proportion of business persons in 15 years, though the numbers have not grown steadily. There is a clearer pattern for the Rajya Sabha, though the observations are only for three time points.

For appreciating the interface between black money, politics and governance, the nature of the transaction in the interface is relevant.

A well-known source of generating black money is corruption in the exercise of decision-making powers to favour or disfavour a group. This is not entirely unusual in many democracies. Of greater direct relevance to the common person is access to public goods, goods to which s/he is entitled. These services (like registering a First Information Report) are often denied unless money changes hands. Petty bureaucracy becomes complicit either out of fear or a need to share the proceeds. These phenomena are not new. One modus operandi of co-opting the bureaucracy in corruption and black money is described by the term 'market for public office' as described by Robert Wade way back in 1985:

> Everyone knows that corruption is common; but there has been little systematic study of the question of how corruption money is used. Everyone knows that public officials are being transferred from post to post very frequently (often with a stay of 12 months or less); but there has been little systematic study of the determinants of transfer or the effects of rapid transfer. And everyone knows that huge amounts of money are typically required to compete for legislative office; but there has been little systematic study of how politicians and parties raise money to finance election battles and nurse constituencies between elections. (p. 468)

Political parties have been known to favour giving election tickets to candidates who are wealthy. These candidates not only contribute to the party coffers, but their capacity to spend more on their own election increases their chances of winning the election. They then have to recover their 'investment'. It is unstated but understood that when elected these representatives will operate the levers of power to recover their investment.

A more recent phenomenon is one of the political leadership itself being attracted to business, thus avoiding transaction costs. The dual roles by the politician and businessman have helped develop close ties, blurring the conflict of interests implicit in their roles. Therefore, whenever the state is empowered to regulate business, it is necessary to recognise that the state apparatus itself has close links with business. Black money facilitates the operation of these links, which no doubt is connected partly to election funding and partly to personal aggrandisement.

The interface between politics, business and government for generation of black money has been facilitated in the recent years by the public–private partnership (PPP) initiative and auction of access to national resource like mining and spectrum. Contracts could be tailor made, modified and not enforced. In the process, the public sector banks came in handy, not only to provide finance on the strength of the PPP contract, but also to end up bearing all the associated financial risks.

SUMMING-UP

The high and rising cost of election expenditure by candidates and political parties and the widely reported use of black money in this expenditure has prompted much discussion of public spending on elections. Government committees in the 1990s also recommended a greater amount of public spending on elections. However, the movement in this direction has been very limited.

In the meanwhile, both the generation and use of black money in politics has been increasing. The entry of candidates of wealth into politics and the movement towards political-cum-business 'entrepreneurship' by individual legislators and political parties has led to politics being soaked with money.

Since spending on elections is much higher than the official ceiling, it is almost entirely in the form of black money. Since the business activities of the political entrepreneurs are through 'close relatives' and benami ownership, there is black money being generated there. The generation of unaccounted money in politics and its use in elections is 'justified' as necessary for being able to meaningfully contest elections.

It is, therefore, not a surprise that Demonetisation 2016 did not see political parties on either side of the divide raising the issue of black money in politics. It would appear that political parties have a stake in the status quo.

Section IV

— *eleven* —

Cash, Money and Liquidity

Demonetisation may be defined as the act of stripping a currency unit of its status as legal tender. The process generally involves exchange of old currency for a new one. On 8 November 2016, the GoI announced that higher denomination currencies, that is, Rs 500 and Rs 1,000, were being demonetised in order to tackle the problems associated with counterfeit currency and black money.

Undoubtedly, the power to demonetise rests with the government, since the currency note is essentially a promissory note issued by the RBI with the guarantee of the GoI and notified as a legal tender by the same. Therefore, the basic decision in this regard lies with the government, the RBI has a substantial stake since it issues the promissory note. It has the responsibility for production, management and circulation of currency.

Once a final decision is taken by the government, the RBI has to implement demonetisation in two steps: namely, accept the demonetised currency and exchange it for remonetised currency through its offices and its agents, namely, branches of banks. The RBI has to incur costs associated with the process. Other things being equal, if the acceptance and exchange takes place simultaneously, there should be little or marginal inconvenience to the citizens and minimal impact on the genuine economic activity. However, if there is a time lag or other considerations, the process of demonetisation may have consequences not associated with demonetisation per se.

The RBI performs several functions, as explained in the appendix 'On the RBI' (at the end of the chapter 'Impact on the Reserve Bank of India'), and currency management is one of them, and a very important one. Demonetisation, depending on how it is managed, has an impact on liquidity management, monetary policy, regulation and its balance sheet.

In the process of Demonetisation 2016, there has been a time lag between the acceptance of old currency and its replacement by a new one. There was also a temporary denial of access to legal currency from the banking system to those who are entitled to it. Obviously, the objective of using information on such exchange for purposes of tracking black money had an impact on the behaviour of economic agents. The magnitudes involved and the geographical spread posed immense logistical challenges. The tasks before the RBI became complex as a result of many factors extraneous to the well understood process of demonetisation. The spillover of the process of demonetisation of currency into monetary management became inevitable. How and why?

CURRENCY, CASH AND MONEY

Demonetisation refers to currency; though currency is the most important component, it is not the only component of money. It is useful, therefore, to appreciate the concepts relevant to demonetisation, namely coins, currency, cash, money, money supply, liquidity and monetary policy.

Money as we understand now, is called fiat money and derives its value by being declared by a government to be legal tender; the government by a fiat declares that it must be accepted as a form of payment within the boundaries of the country, for all debts.

The broad money of a country consists of currency (banknotes and coins), and bank money (the balances held in checking/current accounts, savings accounts, and other types of bank accounts depending on definitions used by the monetary authority). Bank money as part of broad money increases as the economy develops, but it is the facility to use bank money as though it is cash that makes it part of the money supply.

In theory, the main functions of money are described as a medium of exchange; a unit of account; a store of value; and, sometimes, a standard of deferred payment. Any item or verifiable record that fulfils these functions is considered as money in economics. So, money is a broad term that refers to any financial instrument that can fulfil the above-mentioned four functions. In practice, however, it is the status of legal tender that makes currency money.

Money supply is the aggregate amount of financial instruments available for purchasing goods or services within a country. The money supply or amount of money in an economy is measured by adding together all the relevant financial instruments creating a monetary aggregate. The central bank of the country defines the instruments to be included in the computation. In any computation of money supply, cash is the base.

The amount of money actually issued by the central bank of a country is base money. It is measured as currency plus deposits of banks and other institutions with the central bank. What matters is not only the quantity of currency, but also the velocity, namely the number of times it is used for transactions. Money has to be measured as quantity multiplied by velocity (cash stored has the least velocity).

The control of the amount of money in the economy is known as monetary policy. Monetary policy is the process by which a government, the central bank, or the monetary authority manages the supply of money to achieve specific goals. Usually, the goal of monetary policy is to accommodate economic growth in an environment of stable prices and overall financial stability.

Counterfeit currency is imitation currency produced without the legal sanction of the state or government. Producing or using counterfeit money is a form of fraud or forgery.

In English, the word *cash* is derived from the south Indian Dravidian words *kaasu/kasa* meaning money. In southern India, these words continue to be used today, and are referred to money and cash interchangeably. Cash, defined to consist of coins and currency, is the most liquid asset, because it can be 'sold' for goods and services instantly with no loss of value. There is no wait for a suitable buyer of the cash. There is no trade-off between speed and value. It can be used immediately to perform economic actions like buying, selling, or paying debt, meeting immediate wants and needs.

CASH

Cash (notes and coins) is used to make small payments conveniently and promptly, though the latter role is being replaced more and more frequently by electronic payment systems. Cash is becoming a smaller part of the money supply. Its role is being reduced to providing a form of currency storage and payment for only those who do not wish to take part in other systems. Research has found that the demand for cash decreases as debit/credit card usage increases because merchants need not maintain large amounts of cash to provide change for customer purchases.

There is, however, no cashless society. It is still an idea that, in the future, cash will be redundant having been replaced by electronic means of transfer. In the United Kingdom, for instance, only one in seven no longer carry cash. There is a movement towards reduced cash use in an economy, but a cashless society is yet to arrive. With cash, currency is gaining prominence, and within a currency, smaller denominations are in demand for all legitimate transactions.

Cash continues to be relevant and is the most liquid form of money. Banks also create money; in banking, liquidity means the bank's ability to meet obligations when they become due. Managing liquidity is a daily process requiring bankers to monitor and project cash flows to ensure that adequate liquidity is maintained. When a bank cannot discharge its obligations to provide money or cash that it owes others, it means that liquidity has dried up. A central bank has to ensure availability of adequate cash for meeting liquidity needs, and manage appropriate supply of money for the banking system to function. It uses a variety of instruments to influence money supply. In the modern economic system, credit plays a major part. Credit conditions are influenced by the central bank.

In the normal course, currency management involves the supply of currency to meet the demands of society. The printing and disbursement of currency is only one component of supply of money. The aggregate money supply is managed by a central bank through a variety of instruments that affect the non-cash component of money; the part that is dominant. But in the base money, currency remains critical. The critical difference between currency and other forms of money in checking/current accounts is that the former is anonymous, while the latter can be traced and hence the connection with black money—the same quality that renders gold as a store or value for black money.

The central bank releases the cash, but the banking system creates money by lending the deposits it gets to others, which in turn is spent and so on. The money in the economy is thus a multiple of cash and can be considered, for simplicity, as the money multiplier. From the point of transactions, money is used many times, and the times it goes around is called the velocity of circulation.

In times of demonetisation, the liquidity conditions are affected by the process of exchange of old notes with the new ones.

The operations of banks are automatically affected unless the replacement happens with no cost incurred and instantly. In brief, while currency management described in this chapter is the visible side of the work of the RBI, during demonetisation there are several other challenges to RBI in terms of managing money supply, liquidity and credit conditions, as explained later.

CURRENCY MANAGEMENT BY RBI

India is the largest producer and consumer of currency notes, next only to China. Cash plays a dominant role in payments in the country with the banknotes in circulation (in value terms) placed at Rs 16.41 lakh crore as of end of March 2016, their volume being 90.27 billion pieces. The entire planning for designing, printing and distribution of new bank notes (of denominations Rs 2 and above) throughout the country and also withdrawing soiled notes from circulation is the responsibility of the RBI as the currency authority of the country. Currency management is one of RBI's core central banking functions.

The bank notes issued by the RBI are in the nature of promissory notes and are payable 'on demand'. The RBI is under obligation to honour these promissory notes and cannot refuse their exchange in the normal circumstances.

LEGAL TENDER CHARACTER

The legal tender character is granted to the notes issued by the RBI by the provision under Section 26(1) of the RBI Act, which also says that the same is guaranteed by the central government. It is also provided in the subsequent clause [26(2)] that the central government by notification in the Gazette may 'declare that with effect from such date as may be specified in the Notification, any series of bank notes of any denomination shall cease to be legal tender'. The Government shall issue such notification on the recommendations of the central board of the RBI.

The Gazette Notification No. 2652 issued on 8 November 2016 by the GoI fulfils these requirements and, therefore, the legality of the demonetisation decision and the subsequent actions are not an issue.

Further, a question arises as to whether the phrase 'extent to which such notes will be legal tender' used in Section 26(2) of the RBI Act empowers the government to set a time limit on expiry of which the notes will cease to be legal tender even at the offices of the RBI? In other words, will the 'promise to pay' cease and so will the liability of the RBI?

The Supreme Court, while upholding the constitutional validity of demonetisation of rupee notes in January 1978 in the case of *Jayantilal Ratanchand Shah vs. Reserve Bank of India & Others* vide its judgment dated 9 August, 1996 observed,

> On a conspectus of the above provisions of the RBI Act, it is patently clear that Bank is the sole note issuing authority and has the obligation to exchange those notes when demanded except when, and to the extent, it is relieved of that obligation by the Central Government.

The Supreme Court's reading of Section 26(2) of the RBI Act is that the RBI's obligation to exchange the notes on demand can be relieved by the central government. This too supports the cancellation of obligation under the notes that are not surrendered within the prescribed time.

PRINTING AND DISTRIBUTION OF BANK NOTES

The first step in any process of operationalising demonetisation is printing new currency notes and ensuring distribution to the outlets, where they have to be exchanged for old notes.

The RBI places an indent for banknotes with the printing presses on the basis of an econometric model factoring in inter alia, real GDP growth prospects, monetary requirements needed for such growth, rate of inflation and denomination-wise disposal rate of soiled notes. The indents placed by banks are also taken into consideration. The total number of banknotes supplied during 2015–16 by the presses was 21.2 billion pieces against an indent of 23.9 billion pieces.

As per *RBI Annual Report for 2014–15*, about 40 per cent of the currency notes circulated in India are printed by government presses, while the remaining 60 per cent emanate from the RBI currency presses. During 2015–16, The Bharatiya Reserve Bank Note Mudran Private Limited (BRBNMPL), a subsidiary of the RBI, produced 14,714 million pieces of banknotes of different denominations as against its annual target of 15,700 million pieces. However, the RBI imports several of the main ingredients (paper, ink, some of the security features) required for printing currency. The Bank Note Paper Mill India Private Limited (BNPMIPL) in Mysuru, which is a joint venture between BRBNMPL and the Security Printing and Minting Corporation of India Limited (SPMCIL), with a production capacity of 12,000 million tonnes of quality paper, has commenced commercial production.

The RBI discharges its currency functions through the Department of Currency Management at its central office and 19 Issue Departments at its offices located mainly in state capitals. At the other centres, it carries out its functions through the 'currency chests' mechanism. Currency chests are storehouses wherein new, re-issuable and soiled notes are stored along with coins. There are about 4,000 currency chests and 3,700 small coin depots spread across the country through which the RBI carries on its currency functions. They are managed by commercial, cooperative and regional rural banks as agents of the RBI.

The bank notes and coins are put into actual circulation by the vast network of commercial bank branches (about 1,40,000) to whom the RBI supplies new or re-issuable notes based on their indents and actual utilisation in the immediate past. The actual supplies are made from currency chests through a system of remittances to and from the bank branches. Notes and coins withdrawn from circulation are also stored in currency chests till they are sent to RBI for disposal. RBI has also put in place procedures for exchange of soiled and damaged notes.

IN THE AFTERMATH OF THE ANNOUNCEMENT

When demonetisation came into effect from the midnight of 8 November 2016, prima facie, every commercial bank branch as the agent of the RBI, was supposed to be ready to supply new notes either in exchange of old notes or drawals from the accounts from 10 November onwards, subject to the limits prescribed.

The stock position of the notes of various denominations, including the new Rs 500 and Rs 2,000 notes with the RBI, the 4,000 currency chests and the bank branches on the day of announcement is not known. Even assuming that enough stocks were available with the RBI (within its vaults and in currency chests) supplying them in big quantities to as many as 1,40,000 branches of banks spread over all the corners of the country involved a large-scale operation with perfect coordination between the different agencies like railways, road transporters, police, etc. Quite a number of the rural bank branches function in areas which are not easily accessible. No amount of planning would have kept all these branches supplied with enough notes. Hence, whatever supplies they could get, were naturally getting exhausted within hours, and people had to return empty handed despite being in queues for hours which seriously disrupted their normal lives. Recalibration and supplying and maintaining cash stocks with the ATM network (with about 215,000 machines) was going to be equally onerous.

A look at the quantum of notes supplied by RBI (to banks) in the last three years will explain the complexity of the problems better.

TABLE 11.1: Notes in Circulation and New Notes Supplied

(in billions of pieces)

Financial year	*2013–14*	*2014–15*	*2015–16*
No. of notes in circulation at the end of the year	77.33	83.58	90.26
Notes supplied during the year	20.92	23.65	21.20

Source: *RBI Annual Report*, *2015–16*.

The figures show that the RBI was supplying on an average 22 billion pieces of notes to banks during an entire year, which covered all denominations. As of end-March 2016, out of the 90.26 billion pieces of notes in circulation, about 15.7 billion (17.4 per cent of the total) were of Rs 500 denomination. Another 6.3 billion (7 per cent) were of Rs 1,000 denomination. As against this, the presses supplied 4.3 billion pieces of Rs 500 and nearly 1 billion pieces of Rs 1,000 in 2015–16. To remonetise the entire stock of demonetised notes, the presses would have had to produce nearly four times the previous year's production of Rs 500 notes and thrice the production in case of Rs 1,000 (assuming that the Rs 2,000 note would fully replace the Rs 1,000 note). Even if the normal production levels were stepped up and presses worked thrice as much (three shifts against presumably one shift earlier), it would have taken an entire year to remonetise fully. Assuming only two-thirds of the notes are remonetised, the presses would take nine months. This apart, there were challenges of arranging for thrice the amount of paper, ink, etc. in the short period of time available.

It is clear from the above that it would not have been possible for the RBI to keep the banks stocked with as many pieces of notes that too exclusively of higher denomination notes well before or immediately after the announcement. In other words, replacing the 22 billion pieces of high denomination notes in a matter of 30 or 50 days was a Herculean task. The simple fact, which emerges is that neither the RBI nor the commercial banks had the capacity to handle the extraordinary situation to meet the legitimate expectations of the people. The same goes for the capacity to print, which is limited and cannot be stretched beyond a point, especially because of the need to maintain secrecy and other sensitivities involved in the exercise.

IMPORT OF NOTES

There are very few companies in the world which undertake note paper production and printing, and their capacities are usually committed several years in advance to various monetary authorities. It is difficult to find spare capacities within the short span of time available. Further, giving them the new designs and security features is not without risk. The logistics involved and the need to maintain secrecy precluded imports. Even so, the import of additional note paper—as our capacity is limited—also poses challenges in the short period available.

WITHDRAWAL OF NOTES

The tasks associated with the withdrawal of notes is as challenging as those with its distribution. The RBI has to reconcile accounting entries with physical stocks. The physical verification of notes surrendered and sorting the counterfeit and genuine is yet another task. There are financial implications of any mismatch or inappropriate classification. The manpower, equipment and systems are designed for the normal flow and not for managing a flow that happens to be a multiple of the normal and in a short span of time.

The process of demonetisation involves not merely supply of new notes to replace the demonetised ones, but the pieces received have to be accounted for and assessed for their genuineness, virtually branch-wise. Receiving and accounting for them in a short period, almost doubles the workload involved for distributing new notes.

SUMMING-UP

To sum up, demonetisation appears to be a simple process of replacing currency, but the magnitudes and time-frame for the task placed a great burden on the RBI. But, the banking system as a whole had to engage itself in the task of demonetisation. Hence, the banking system was not in a position to perform the normal functions that create bank money in a smooth manner. The supply of both cash and money was constrained with a multiplier effect on demand and supply for money.

To put it briefly, the task assigned to the RBI was such that great pain was, perhaps, inevitable.

— *twelve* —

Impact on the Banking System

The banking system is critical for the execution of the process of demonetisation. The responsibility for executing the process after the November 2016 demonetisation fell squarely on the banking system as an extended arm of the RBI, or as its agency for conducting several functions. Banks do, in the normal course, operate currency chests, move cash to branches, exchange the currency or accept deposits after following due procedures. On receipt of old notes, they scrutinise the currency for counterfeiting, classify, reconcile accounts and finally bear the losses in case there are discrepancies. They, thus, receive new notes from the RBI and transmit the used or surrendered ones to the central bank.

In the normal course, there would have been a mere exchange of new and old currencies. In the 2016 demonetisation, the process involved unprecedented magnitudes, the time lag between the surrender of old and release of new currency added to the pressure. In addition, there were inadequate quantities of currency of legal tender for several days to meet the demand for new currency. As a result, the banks could not discharge their normal obligation of withdrawal of deposits made.

Operations

The magnitude of transactions and number of people the banks interacted with was a multiple of what it did under normal circumstances. The capacity of the system was stretched. In addition to the volumes and complexities, such as adhering to 'KYC' norms and ascertaining the genuineness of the currency, the operations had to be conducted in an emotionally charged atmosphere. The bankers had to incur the wrath of the customers for not being able to get back the money they had deposited. They had to manage 'crowds'—a challenge that they were neither trained in to handle nor accustomed to. The Indian Banks' Association, which often provides guidelines, was conspicuous by its silence. The RBI's instructions were often released to the press before they were communicated to the branches, and the staff had to wait for official confirmation. This further annoyed the customers. Adverse publicity about a few incidents involving fraud added to the agony of the bankers. In particular, the bankers felt that some of the raids and other actions did not distinguish between genuine errors due to pressure of work and fraud.

The major failure of the banking industry was in operating the ATMs. The industry was, perhaps, too slow to respond adequately and ensure withdrawals within the constraints imposed by the RBI. Yet the general feeling among the bankers was that it was a process with a laudable objective and worthy of patience and dedication.

Costs and Benefits

The banking system had to bear costs associated with the process. Transporting and auditing a far larger amount of cash than the normal meant a higher cost of transportation, insurance and security. Additional staff and working overtime became necessary. The cost of genuine mistakes such as those in identifying counterfeit reconciliation, etc. also became high. Several system-related charges, such as the use of ATMs, debit cards, etc. increased due to configuration or restrictions imposed by the government. Reporting requirements were also onerous. There was no indication of tangible benefits to the banking system by either the government or the RBI. Though, over time, there was an awareness of potential benefits to the banking system in terms of a larger deposit base, lending opportunities and lower inflation as well as interest rates.

SHORT-TERM IMPACT

Banks had to reckon with huge increases in deposits. The work on several other aspects of banking was neglected. The servicing of loans and payment of interest and principal due was often delayed either due to disruption of activity or as a result of the impact on commercial viability. Regulatory forbearance such as those relating to income recognition and asset classification provided marginal relief. Credit growth, which was already sluggish, was almost under partial suspension.

BEYOND TEMPORARY IMPACT

It is expected that demonetisation by reducing the role of cash would contribute positively to the growth of banking. Even if half of the deposit growth is retained, it would augment bank-intermediation of transactions in the economy. A lower cost of funds, and hence a potential increase in lending opportunities is observable. The stock market valuation of shares in public sector banks points to a positive impact beyond the short term.

The most challenging task for the banking system is to replace the credit needs of the economic activities that were in the past met through cash out of black money. To the extent the stock of such cash has been transferred to the banks from the informal channels, the banks have to find means of extending credit. The existing institutional arrangements and procedures do not permit them.

Perhaps, banks have to expand their reach through Non-bank Financial Institutions (NBFIs) and even Banking Correspondents.

ISSUES

The banking industry and the employees have, on the whole, participated in the process, with more dedication and less disgust than was anticipated or reported in the media. Yet, there are two issues that remain matters of concern.

Has the much promised and long overdue autonomy of public sector banking been compromised? Demonetisation by itself is unlikely to have any impact on the autonomy of the public sector banks since it has never been granted despite the recommendations of commissions in 1991 and 1998, and subsequent assurances by the government.

Has denial of cash that belonged to the customers, kept with banks for a prolonged period, had an impact on trust in banking? There has been anger and frustration among people, but trust in the banking industry remains unaffected by demonetisation, and this despite other reasons like rising non-performing assets, which adversely affects the image of the banks.

— *thirteen* —

Impact on the Reserve Bank of India

The RBI is responsible for production, issue, circulation and destruction of currency. It is, therefore, central to the process of carrying out the process of demonetisation, namely substitution of old currency with new ones. The process initiated in November 2016 impacts it in several ways. The impacts are on the income and expenditure, balance sheet, transfers to government, monetary policy, liquidity, regulation of banks, payment system and reputation.

Income-Expenditure

Most of the income earned by the RBI is from interest earnings of domestic assets and foreign securities, while most of the expenditure is incurred on three items: printing of notes, employees, and agency charges (that is, payments to the banks for performing functions as banker to governments on behalf of the RBI). Table 13.1 illustrates the position of current income-expenditure management, and treatment of surplus over transfer of reserves.

In 2015–16, the RBI spent Rs 3,421 crore on printing notes. Expenditure on this account will naturally be higher as a result of demonetisation. There may, if at all, be a marginal increase in employee cost on this account. Since 2013–14, 99.99 per cent of the surplus of income over expenditure is being transferred; for example, Rs 65,876 crore in 2015–16 to the government.

In sum, the additional cost of printing will, in effect, be borne by the government via reduced surplus transferred to government.

TABLE 13.1: Income and Expenditure of RBI for 2015–16

(Rs in crore)

1.	Income	80,870
	Of which interest	74,924
2.	Expenditure	14,990
	Of which Printing	3,421
3.	Available balance	65,880
	Of which surplus paid to Government	65,876

Source: *Annual Report of Reserve Bank of India 2015–16.*

In the medium to long term, if the currency to deposit ratio comes down significantly, there may be savings in printing costs.

ASSETS AND LIABILITIES

In the normal course, demonetisation implies replacement of old currency with the new. With 100 per cent replacement, there is no impact on assets or liabilities of RBI. However, in the current context, there has been an expectation that a significant amount of currency notes will not turn up for replacement and may not be deposited in the banks. To that extent, the liabilities of RBI will be reduced.[1]

[1] In the unlikely event of the number of old currency notes offered for exchange exceeds those on the record of the RBI, there will be increase in liabilities of the RBI. Hence that has to be provided for, implying an increased expenditure on this account. This situation would arise only if there has been miscalculation, or if the RBI accepts as counterfeit currencies sent through the banking system because the security features of such currency happen to be in total alignment with genuine currency.

In the initial stages of the process of demonetisation, there was an expectation that significant amounts of unaccounted money will get extinguished, but by 10 December a large amount (Rs 12.44 lakh crore or trillion) had already entered the banking system. Under the circumstances, it is unlikely that there will be a significant reduction in liabilities. However, there would be a fiscal gain of 75 per cent from the amounts declared under the new amnesty scheme. A clear picture of unaccounted money that has been manipulated to escape the attention of the tax authorities through the process will emerge only after investigations are completed.

The question that has been debated in the context of demonetisation is whether the extinguished liability of the RBI in terms of notes that were demonetised, but not remonetised, represents windfall gains to the RBI and thus could be transferred to the government to support its fiscal position.

In the initial phase of this debate, a distinction was sought to be made between the withdrawal of the legal tender character of the demonetised notes and the extinguishment of the liability. The argument was that the 8 November notification under Section 26(2) merely withdrew the legal tender character, and that the liability of the RBI continued unless specifically extinguished. Many held that in the light of the Supreme Court decision in 1978, there is no need for any legislative approval for the extinguishment of the liability and that the Section 26(2) notification serves the purpose. Others said that there is need for some form of legislative approval to withdraw the promise to pay on the currency note. The example of the European Commercial Bank (ECB) was quoted when the Euro was introduced and that of the Bank of England when it withdrew the legal tender character of the old 50 pound note. Eventually, the government brought in an ordinance on 30 December 2016 to extinguish the liability and put the matter beyond doubt.

As per normal accounting practice, any liability that is no longer on the balance sheet can be transferred either to the reserve account or distributed to the owner as profit. So, the government as sole owner stands to gain to the extent notes have not been exchanged within the time limits indicated in the legal notification and the ordinance. But, the accounting practices of central banks are not uniform though general principles are recognised. There are two considerations in taking a view on treatment of windfall gain. First, transactions between the RBI and the government by themselves are internal to the public sector, when a consolidated view of balance sheets of the central bank and government is taken.

Second, and more important, generally balance sheet objectives drive operations of institutions, but in the case of the RBI, policy objectives drive operations and balance sheet effects reflect the results. So, the RBI as the monetary authority pursues its objectives, irrespective of the impact on the balance sheet, and in case its capital is eroded, it requires implicit replenishment from the government. Hence, the treatment of windfall gains by the RBI and the government would be driven more by macro policy considerations than mere accounting principles. Where the GoI and the RBI differ, in the final analysis, it will be the government that prevails; in any case the RBI's balance sheet is part of the public sector.

TREATMENT OF WINDFALL GAINS

Keeping in view the unique characteristics of the balance sheet of the RBI, a wide range of options for treatment of windfall gains has been suggested. The first one is to reduce the assets of the RBI in the form of government securities. This implies debt cancellation and it is a prudent option. The second option is to transfer the surplus to the RBI reserves, thereby strengthening its balance sheet for any future contingency. The third is clearly a dividend transfer to the government supporting fiscal management in the ensuing year. A combination of any or more of these three options is also possible.

Debt cancellation will have only a marginal impact on the fisc as the extent of interest expenditure saved will be more or less matched by the reduction in income transferred from the RBI on account of lower earnings due to cancellation of government debt held by it. This, of course, assumes that normally the RBI would transfer almost all of its earnings on government securities each year to the GoI. There will be a monetary impact as there is a reduction in reserve money to the extent of debt cancellation, but there is also a view that these operations will be reserve money neutral. If, in the view of the RBI, the system needs liquidity to be injected to replace the currency left without remonetisation, it could do so through appropriate open market operations. In this option, the windfall gains are in effect used to reduce government debt, but only the debt owed to the RBI. The debt to GDP ratio would, to that extent, be lower.

Transfer to the RBI's reserve, the second option, has no immediate impact on the fisc as none of the windfall gains are transferred to the GoI, but the addition to reserves in future may be avoided. For the economy, there is a positive impact if the strengthening of the RBI's balance sheet is perceived as a positive signal. However, as illustrated from Table 13.2, since 2013–14, the government and the RBI have used all the surplus of income over expenditure to support the fisc and not the balance sheet of the RBI.

The third option, transfer to the government as special dividend, transfers windfall gain to the government, the owner. The government can use these gains either to reduce the deficit to the extent of gains transferred by retiring its debt, or it can increase expenditure without increasing its deficit.

TABLE 13.2: Trends in Income, Expenditure and Net Disposable Income of the RBI

(Rs in billion)

Item	*2011–12*	*2012–13*	*2013–14*	*2014–15*	*2015–16*
Income	531.76	743.58	646.17	792.56	808.70
Total expenditure	261.51	455.63	646.17	792.56	808.70
Surplus transfer to the government	160.10	330.10	526.79	658.96	658.76
Transfer of surplus to government as per cent of Gross Income less Total Expenditure	37.20	53.40	99.99	99.99	99.99

Source: *Annual Report of Reserve Bank of India 2015–16.*

On the monetary side, if the GoI increases it expenditure to the extent of the transfer, there will be neutral impact on liquidity, except that the liquidity in hands of the public in the form of demonetised currency is now replaced by liquidity in the hands of the government. On the other hand, if the government reduces its fiscal deficit using the special dividend, the extent of market borrowing will be reduced with liquidity released for use by the public. Whether the government reduces its deficit or increases its expenditure, the monetary impact is neutral and in both cases the public has more liquidity equivalent to the extinguished currency, indirectly from the budget in one case, and directly through lower market borrowing in the other.

The choices between or a combination of three routes should be based on the needs of overall monetary and fiscal management. This will also depend to an extent on the stock of unaccounted money that comes into the banking system.[2]

[2] The amount of black money in the demonetised currencies that does not enter the banking system—that is, the black money that is

MONETARY POLICY

The withdrawal of the legal tender character of the Rs 500 and Rs 1,000 notes on 8 November 2016 without prompt and full replacement, created a severe cash crunch and affected all sectors of the economy that were cash-intensive. These involved construction, small businesses, especially in the informal sector, transport, and trade more so in perishables like vegetables and fruits. The RBI had to modulate its monetary policy of 7 December 2016 taking into account the impact on growth and prices and taking a call on whether the drop in the level of activity would be short or medium term. It revised the growth forecast for 2016–17 down from 7.6 per cent to 7.1—'mainly due to slower growth in cash intensive and unorganized sectors as the wealth effect was expected to be limited'.

Since then there have been various forecasts of economic growth. There have also been views expressed that food prices will pose risks as the farm sector has been impacted—but that this will show up with a lag. As more data and anecdotal information becomes available, the RBI will have to calibrate its monetary policy.

---

extinguished—will reduce the liability of the central bank to the same extent, and will be a 100 per cent capital gain for the RBI. The black money that is deposited in the banks and declared under the second 2016 amnesty scheme will, under the terms of the scheme, see the government obtaining 75 per cent (including the 25 per cent that is to be kept in non-interest bearing deposits) and the holder of black money keeping 25 per cent. The remaining stock of black money that is deposited in the banks, but is neither declared nor detected is most likely to be money that has successfully circumvented the application of the law. It is not inconceivable that this portion could move out of the banking system and return to the black economy.

In the normal course, demonetisation would mean an instant exchange of currency, but this was not the case with the 8 November 2016 demonetisation. Hence, the immediate impact of demonetisation has been a huge rise in the deposits in the banking system. Substantively, money as measured by cash plus bank deposits remained unaffected, but there was shortage of legal tender liquidity in the economic system and excess of liquidity in the banking system.

A cost had to be incurred to drain the excess liquidity from the banking system. All the instruments for such operations at the disposal of the RBI and the government had to be used, namely the Market Stabilisation Scheme (MSS), open market operations and the Cash Reserve Ratio (CRR), imposing a corresponding burden on the government, RBI and banking system, respectively.[3]

In the short term, the only option with banks flush with liquidity was to place funds with the RBI through reverse repos and buy bonds. The 10 year GoI bond which was 6.8 per cent on 7 November dropped by 60 bps to 6.2 as the deposits started growing with the banks. On 26 November 2016, the RBI brought in incremental CRR to impound the excess liquidity in the system. The GoI approved the RBI's proposal for an increase in the limit for the MSS. This provided the RBI with the armoury to conduct open market operations in a smooth manner and it could withdraw the incremental CRR. Yields softened as the RBI became proactive in liquidity management.

---

[3]Each of these three instruments is distinct. Under the MSS, the government bears the interest cost though it does not use the proceeds. Under the Open Market Operations, the RBI buys and sells government securities in the market and it bears the cost of servicing these securities. Under the CRR, banks have to maintain a certain proportion of their deposits with the RBI. Interest is not paid on the deposits maintained with the RBI. So the cost of the CRR is borne by the banks.

REGULATION

The process of demonetisation, due to its scale, design and implementation had disrupted normal economic activity for several days. Hence, regulatory actions were warranted both for smooth implementation of demonetisation and for moderating the consequences of disruptions caused in the banking system.

Exemptions were granted for using the demonetised notes for certain purposes up to 30 November 2016, including repayment of loans to commercial and cooperative banks. However, such exemption was not extended to loans taken from the Non-Banking Financial Corporations (NBFC), including from the micro-finance institutions (MFIs). As the NBFC and MFI sectors cover a large number of borrowers in the informal sector, the denial of the exemption to use the old notes for repayment created fears of overdues building up in this sector. The RBI announced an extension of 60 days time for repayment of loans by small borrowers defined as those with limits up to Rs 1 crore.

From the regulatory perspective, the RBI treated District Central Co-operative Banks (DCCBs) differently and did not allow these banks to accept old notes as deposits or provide exchange facility for these notes, while the other categories of banks including urban cooperative banks and state cooperative banks were allowed to do so.

The disruption caused by demonetisation meant that many borrowers could not service their loans taken from banks. So, regulatory forbearance was required in terms of classification of assets as sub-standard and recognition as a non-performing asset.

PAYMENT SYSTEM

The demonetisation process had an immediate effect of resulting in a substantial flow into bank deposits and the use of technology for transactions. It is likely to have an impressive impact on the integrity of financial transactions across the board. It will also provide information on a far larger mass of financial transactions than before and thus improve the integrity of the financial sector. The use of technology in the payment system is also likely to add to the efficiency of the payment system and minimise the cost of transactions. Further, with reduced reliance on cash, there is likely to be less demand on currency from the RBI resulting in overall savings in printing of notes.

RISKS

Broadly speaking, risks faced by central banks can be divided into financial and non-financial. To some extent, the level of capital and reserves provides comfort in relation to financial risks. In the recent years, there has virtually been no addition to the reserves of the RBI, though the size of the balance sheet has expanded, as explained earlier in this chapter. As a result, there has been a prima facie dilution of the reserve adequacy since 2013–14, and hence a potential dent to the financial independence of the RBI.

Among the non-financial risks, operational risks rank high; and bank note printing and delivery operations affect large segments of the population. In managing the demonetisation processes, it is not clear whether the operational risks were fully evaluated before deciding and launching the process. Similarly, it is not clear whether the Central Board of the RBI evaluated the policy risks in recommending demonetisation.

Above all, the decision, the design and the implementation of demonetisation by all accounts, posed reputational risks to the RBI. There is anecdotal evidence that the reputation of the RBI has, in fact, got dented.

Of all the risks, reputational risks should be of the greatest concern to any central bank.[4] It can arise not only of its own volition, but also for factors beyond the central bank's control and these cannot be ignored. Communication, especially in the media is an integral part of managing such risks.

That demonetisation has dented the image of the RBI has been noted by a journal.[5] Fortunately, a rating agency, noting

---

[4] The Bank of International Settlements (2009) has observed, 'Overarching the categories of financial, operational and policy risk is reputational risk. Reputational risk can be viewed as secondary, in that reputational damage usually is caused by a loss or failure in the areas of policy, operations or finance. But given the importance of credibility to central banks, reputational damage can be their greatest concern. In a 2003 BIS survey (...), the vast majority of respondents reflected the view that continued reliance on the central bank as an independent authority with the necessary financial resources ultimately depends on trust in the institution.

'Reputational risks can occur when there is a mismatch between public perceptions and the actual objectives and resources of the central bank. Serious misconduct, human or system failures or major difficulties in meeting objectives are not frequent among the central banks, but they can seriously damage credibility when they do occur. Questions concerning ethical conduct and core principles such as honesty and integrity can pose a more severe test than purely legal issues, such as litigation against the organisation,' P. 154.

[5] *The Economist* in an article on 3 December wrote: 'India's economy will eventually recover and may even gain strength: the forced priming of bank accounts and the switch to electronic payments will mobilise more money for lending and taxes. But there may be lasting damage to institutions, most notably the RBI itself. It failed, among other things, to warn the impatient Mr Modi that there were not enough new notes to replace old ones. It has issued a bewildering blitz of complex and sometimes contradictory instructions to banks. Its governor, Urjit Patel, has been perplexingly silent. Its reputation for probity, competence and independence is in tatters.'

that a shadow has been cast, concluded that 'it's a very mature institution'.[6] The RBI's image has been dented, but not beyond repair.

[6] A Reuter's news item on 15 December 2016 reporting the comments of Standard and Poor through its Director Kyran Curry noted, 'Curry, in a teleconference with media, said demonetisation had undermined confidence in the predictability and effectiveness of policymaking in India, including of the RBI. Demonetisation has cast a shadow over the RBI's competence and independence', Curry said.

However, he also noted, 'We still think this institution is a very credible one, and in terms of the conduct of monetary policy, it's a very mature institution'.

Appendix

On the RBI

Through the Reserve Bank of India Act 1935, and some other legislations, the government has entrusted select responsibilities to the RBI with necessary freedom to carry them out. This has been done to ensure that important matters relating to money and finance are perceived by the common person as being performed by an independent and professional body. To be effective, the RBI has to convince the people that it is acting in its own best judgement: but, at the same time, in a parliamentary democracy, it has to be accountable to Parliament through the Ministry of Finance.

The RBI touches lives of people in many important ways that are seldom realised. Prices matter to everyone, and so does the value of money. Interest rates matter to depositors and borrowers, and, in fact, for financing growth and employment. Financial transactions involve banks and clearance of cheques, or more broadly, payment systems. The RBI is the banker to the government and, thus, ease of all financial transactions by individuals and corporates with the government is facilitated by the central bank. The exchange rate is of concern for many, especially the millions of students and Non-Resident Indian (NRI) workers. Above all, the RBI's functioning is relevant to anyone who uses currency that it produces and makes available, and the coins that it distributes on behalf of the government.

The Reserve Bank of India Act was placed on the statute book in March 1934, though it became operational on April 1st 1935. In 1913, John Maynard Keynes, easily amongst the most noted economists in history, was one among many who addressed this issue and proposed a 'State Bank' in 1913 to be owned by the government and performing both central banking and commercial banking functions. Work on legislation for establishment of a central bank was, however, initiated in January 1927, but the Reserve Bank of India Bill was finally introduced in September 1933 and enacted in 1934. At that time, Burma (now Myanmar) was part of India and currency notes issued by the RBI had the denomination shown in Burmese language also. It was a private shareholder bank till it was nationalised and became a government-owned one in 1949. According to the Preamble of the Act, 'In the present disorganisation of the monetary systems of the world it is not possible to determine what will be suitable as a permanent basis for the Indian monetary system'; and hence the Act was 'to make temporary provision on the basis of the existing monetary system, and to leave the question of the monetary standard best suited to India to be considered when the international monetary position has become sufficiently clear and stable to make it possible to frame permanent measures'. Obviously, the international monetary system has continued to be neither 'clear' nor 'stable'; and so we continue to be governed by this temporary provision, which according to many, if not all, has served the nation well. The humility of the lawmakers of that time is admirable though.

As per the Act, the bank is obliged to have offices at four places, viz., Madras, Calcutta, Bombay and Delhi. The Central Office of the RBI was initially established in Calcutta, but was permanently moved to Mumbai in 1937.

The RBI's affairs are governed by a Central Board of Directors, fourteen of them, and all are nominated by the government. This includes the official Directors, viz. Governor and not more than four Deputy Governors, and two serving government officials, usually the Secretary, Economic Affairs and Secretary, Financial Services. The serving government officials nominated by the government and Deputy Governors can participate, but have no right to vote in the Board. Functions relating to financial supervision are performed under the guidance of the Board of Financial Supervision, which has four Directors of the Central Board as members, in addition to the Governor and Deputy Governors. There are four Local Boards for four regions of India, and one of the members of each Local Board is also a member of the Central Board. All members are appointed by the government. The Local Boards are essentially advisory in nature, and have review and monitoring functions relevant to the region. Salaried government officials cannot be nominated to the Central or Local Boards.

More important, the Governor and in his absence, the Deputy Governor, nominated by him on this behalf will also have powers that the Central Board exercises. In a way, this provides parallel authority to the Governor to conduct the affairs of the RBI unless the Central Board makes regulations limiting such power to exercise all the powers of the Central Board.

The government has a right to give directions to the bank in public interest which is a standard provision in almost all public institutions, but in the case of the RBI, only after consultation with its chief executive, namely, the Governor of the bank. The provision relating to consultation with the Governor is unique to the RBI, and strengthens the position of Governor as its chief executive.

There are other enactments which are administered by the RBI by virtue of the appropriate legislative provisions. Among these, the most important relate to regulation of banks, regulation of foreign exchange, and Payments and Settlements Systems. There are a number of other Acts which are relevant to the functioning of the RBI, and of them the most significant one is the Indian Coinage Act.

The core function of the RBI as per the Act, relates to formulation, implementation and monitoring of Monetary Policy. The objective in this regard is maintaining price stability and ensuring an adequate flow of credit to productive sectors. Second, it manages the foreign exchange inflows and outflows in addition to maintaining reserves in foreign exchange and a sustainable balance of payments. The main objective in this regard is to facilitate external trade and payments. Third, as regulator and supervisor of the financial system, it prescribes broad parameters of banking operations, including licensing of banks within which the country's banking and financial system functions. The objectives are to maintain public confidence in the system, protect depositors' interest and provide cost-effective banking services to the public. The tasks cover ensuring banks are prudent in their operations, adequate competition and protection of consumer interests. Fourth, it issues and exchanges or destroys currency in addition to distribution of coins. The objective is to give to the public adequate quantity of supply of currency notes and coins of acceptable quality to facilitate transactions. Fifth, it has from its very inception accepted a developmental role. This included rural credit, and in addition, establishment of several institutions that were pre-cursors to UTI, IDBI, NABARD (National Bank for Agriculture and Rural Development), etc. Finally, it provides important services to the government. As a banker to the government, it provides banking services to both, central and state governments. It performs many of these functions through its agents, namely, banks authorised for the purpose. It is also a banker to banks. While the RBI Act gives the right to manage debt of the Union government to the RBI, all the states have entered into an agreement with the RBI to make use of these services.

The Governor is assisted by Deputy Governors, and the law permits up to four of them to be appointed by the government, in effect by the Prime Minister and the Finance Minister. The government may remove from office the Governor or a Deputy Governor. The maximum tenure at the time of appointment is five years, but services may be terminated at any time without assigning any reasons.

— *fourteen* —

Demonetisation, Black Money and Gold

Demonetisation is the process of removing a currency from general usage or circulation. The process as understood in the current context relates to the status of currency notes of specified denominations issued in the past by the RBI. Gold is a commodity and hence a process dealing with currency should have no relevance to it. Demonetisation 2016 is being used for, among other things, fighting against black money. Black money is concerned with money that is not accounted for tax purposes. Gold is not integral to either demonetisation or black money, and yet the subject became part of the events in connection with the November 2016 demonetisation. The main reason is that though gold is not money, it has some characteristics of money, essentially as a store of value and to a very limited extent as a medium of exchange. Gold is, no doubt, a form in which some stock of black money is held in India.

How many black economy transactions take place with gold as a medium? Perhaps a small share, since it is not a unit of account and relative to cash is messy to handle for the purposes of transaction. Gold is more liquid than real estate and easy to hide, but far less liquid and more difficult to handle than cash.

How much stock of black money is held in gold? While there are no estimates, it may not be large relative to real estate and black money taken and held or invested abroad.

Much of the gold stock of India is in the form of gold jewellery held by millions of households. Only that part of gold which is held in non-jewellery forms such as gold bars or coins can be of relevance to transactions relating to black money.

How much of the gold stock held in India could be unaccounted for? It is well known that the appetite for gold in India is large and persistent both as an investment and consumption good (used but with no depletion in the process). It is most likely that gold bars and gold coins are used for investment purposes and may include black money. This may not be a significant part of the total stock of gold. Yet, gold gained the attention of policymakers in the context of demonetisation and black money.

CURRENT JUNCTURE

Immediately after demonetisation was announced on 8 November 2016, there was a rush to buy jewellery. Gold prices surged from Rs 31,000 to Rs 51,000. Media reports suggest that 100 tonnes of gold was imported in November after the announcement of demonetisation, and the purchases were made with demonetised Rs 500 and Rs 1,000 notes.

In brief, the traders in jewellery were operating as instruments for converting what apparently was black money into white. The target of attention, monitoring and action should have been the jewellery traders. Since the sale proceeds have to be deposited in a bank, any extraordinary increases in sales by individual jewellers, is monitorable. The KYC guidelines imposed on the traders in jewellery should serve the purpose of gathering information that demonetisation is expected to give.

In response to the obviously one-off reaction to demonetisation, a one-time event or once in a life-time event, the government gave several clarifications as follows, 'The jewellery or gold purchased out of disclosed income or out of exempted income like agricultural income or out of reasonable household savings or legally inherited which has been acquired out of explained sources is neither chargeable to tax under the existing provisions nor under the proposed amended provisions', the Central Board of Direct Taxes (CBDT) said.

The Finance Ministry in a statement said, 'There is no limit on holding of gold jewellery or ornaments by anybody provided it is acquired from explained sources of income including inheritance.'

The statement added, 'Jewellery and ornaments to the extent of 500gm for married lady, 250gm for unmarried lady and 100gm for male member will not be seized, even if prima facie, it does not seem to be matching with the income record of the assessee.'

Legitimate holding of jewellery up to any extent is fully protected was the definitive clarification. The government said, '... officers conducting search have discretion not to seize even higher quantity of gold jewellery based on factors including family customs and traditions.'

The clarifications were warranted by the importance of gold and gold policy in the country.

Gold has a very special place in Indian society. Gold policy in independent India has a long history of misguided policy that encouraged gold smuggling and generated black money. The current controversies have to be considered against this background.

GOLD IN INDIAN SOCIETY

The demand for gold in India has been a historically recognised fact and has persisted over the centuries. There was a reference to the imports of gold in the discussions among senators of the Roman Empire. Senators complained that Romans were importing many commodities from India and paying for it with valuable gold that they had to acquire. In other words, the demand for gold in many ways is a part of the tradition and culture in India.

As noted earlier, the demand for gold arises both as a consumption good (when gold jewellery is used) and as an investment good (when it can be sold and till then kept as a form of savings). In a way, it is in many, if not all, cases, both an investment good and a consumption good.

In view of the traditional attachment to gold, the aggregate demand for gold increases with the increase in population and income. Hence, in the absence of a drastic change in tradition, there is an understandable persistent increase in demand for gold, almost all of which is to be met through import of gold for jewellery.

In addition, it has been observed that in a few cases, investors invest in gold if they find that equity markets are sluggish or bank interest rates are low. However, there is significant anecdotal evidence to show that gold is also used to some extent for stocking black or unaccounted money. These are often in the form of gold bars or coins.

In brief, therefore, a large part of demand for gold is tradition-based, and some part of it for other reasons, especially as an alternative to investment in financial sector and, to some extent, to store black money. It is necessary to note those gold-traded funds and other financial instruments to mimic investments in gold have not been very successful, indicating that the demand for gold purely for investment of non-black money has been rather low.

For policy purposes, merely because demand for gold is traditional, it does not mean that it is irrational or undesirable. Most of the traditional demand for gold originates from women in India, and this has to be appreciated in the context of an absence of property rights for women on par with men in most of India. Even if there are equal property rights in law, women cannot in reality exercise them. Traditionally, gold is inherited among women. Women are deprived of their gold only under desperate circumstances. Gold provides safety and security for women, and under difficult circumstances, liquidity. It has a special status for women in their relations with other members of the family. Information on gold jewellery holdings by women is exclusive to women. It is significantly non-depreciating in its physical form and in terms of value. It may appear inappropriate to discourage import of gold that meets the needs of women, while the import of luxury cars and men's shaving lotions is permitted freely. The policy for gold should not imply a bias against tradition or a bias in gender.

GOLD POLICY

Demand for gold is both from honest tax-paying or tax-exempt citizens in lower middle classes and middle classes, and to some extent, by those who want to store black money. Black money is closely related to the gold market in India, to the extent a part of gold demand or supply may be dealing with black money. There is a moralistic rather than realistic attitude towards gold in our governance systems, while most of the demand for gold is rooted in our culture and tradition.

The evolution of gold policy since independence centred around five main objectives, viz., to wean people away from gold; regulate its supply; reduce smuggling; reduce demand; and, reduce the domestic price of gold. The first major effort to mobilise the vast gold reserves in the country was the issue of 15-year Gold Bonds at 6.5 per cent in November 1962. To control the diversion of savings into the bullion market, gold control rules were promulgated in January 1963. Control over internal trade and distribution of gold was fully established in 1964. A second attempt was made to issue Gold Bonds in 1980.

Gold Bonds designated as National Defence Gold Bonds was issued in October 1965. The Voluntary Disclosure Scheme (VDS) of 1975 granted immunity from the Gold Control Act. In 1978–79, gold auctions were undertaken as an anti-inflationary measure and to curb smuggling. These were discontinued expeditiously. A Gold Bond scheme was launched in 1993, which garnered 41 tonnes of gold, easily the highest mobilised among all the Gold Bond schemes till then. There was a Gold Deposit Scheme in 1999, and it yielded insignificant amounts.

A number of expert committees have looked into this issue. These include a committee headed by I. G. Patel, the RBI Governor in 1978. It is interesting to note that the Committee said, 'The question of issuing Gold Bond was examined, but not favoured since this would in effect amount to indexing the value of the savings of those who want gold as a hedge against inflation, as compared to the savers who are willing to hold other financial assets.' Subsequently, a working group to review gold policy was appointed in 1986 under the chairmanship of Dr. C. Rangarajan. The RBI came out with a discussion paper in 1992 on this subject. A suggestion was made to set up a Gold Bank with the objective of mobilising domestic non-official gold holdings, and channelise them into a centralised pool over a period of time, and deploy them in a productive manner for the development of the country. However, this was not accepted.

The gold policy was reviewed as part of the reform process after the balance of payment crisis in 1991. It was noted that the import of gold was virtually prohibited for years before the crisis, and yet the crisis occurred. There was a realisation that all efforts to curb smuggling of gold were almost totally ineffective. Large-scale smuggling of gold was possible only by paying for it through unofficial channels. It meant that the policies in regard to the foreign exchange rates of the Rupee get undermined by the unofficial channels of importing gold and financing of such imports. Hence, a decision was taken to officially recognise gold imports so that international transactions relating to gold also become a part of the foreign exchange markets and are thus amenable to policy intervention by the RBI. It is against this background that import of gold was permitted freely. However, import had to be mainly through authorised banks only, and a nominal duty was levied on imports. The import of gold was permitted through select banks and the Metals and Minerals Corporation of India (MMTC), at a nominal duty. The policy has continued since then with occasional temporary increases in duty or other restrictions. So, here is an interesting reform where import of gold was liberalised as a solution to balance of payments problems with the incidental benefit of drastic elimination of an important component of the black economy.

In 2015, the GoI launched three schemes, viz. the Gold Coin Scheme, the Gold Monetisation Scheme and issue of Sovereign Gold Bonds. The three schemes introduced in November 2015 were a landmark in the sense that the government attempted to devise those schemes that meet different needs of the consumers. These together have been described as path-breaking, but they did not have the intended impact.

REACTIONS

The series of clarifications issued by the Finance Ministry on this subject helped clarify matters, but reactions have been intense and widespread. Here is an illustrative response from women taxpayers,

> If the Income Tax officials decide to harass the individual even on account of genuine lack of understanding of ornaments, it is extremely difficult to prove them as inherited ornaments. Inherited jewels are often exchanged for new ones. There is seldom a practise of keeping records.
>
> Even otherwise, it is difficult to prove if they are bought from savings or agricultural income because traditionally except in

very recent times there were rarely bills or receipts given to the customer. And even in recent times not all of them give receipts.

And rarely does anyone write wills for jewellery, and with the result many genuine and innocent citizens could be unfairly taxed and harassed.

Law-abiding citizens may have carefully preserved their ancestral ornaments or kept aside a portion of their savings every year to invest in what they thought as a safe and pleasurable investment for themselves and their children. We don't really understand how all this can be proven in the case of ornament gold.

The solution may be to just investigate very high volume purchases only during the demonetisation period with all jewellers, which may be possible and practical. Or to investigate people who have stocked up on Gold bars. The source for these purchases is easier to find out though not fool proof.

Is it fair to intrude into the privacy of women's jewellery in India, where a wife is not required to disclose to her husband the jewellery she has?

Because of the incompetence or unwillingness of tax authorities to catch those indulging in black money, who may be 10 per cent of the population, what right does the Government have to subject the 90 per cent of ordinary womenfolk to undue stress?

Another fear for law-abiding citizens is the question of the extent of the power of the government to take sweeping arbitrary decisions intruding into our privacy. What may be the legal opinion on this?

SUMMING-UP

Gold has some characteristics of money; but its close association with black money, in the minds of policymakers, generated controversies in the context of demonetisation. However, in Indian society, gold has a special significance. Hence, gold as a form of black money should be curbed while not attacking gold jewellery as a form of women's assets and rights. It is not easy to make this distinction and design policies and procedures accordingly. Tackling other forms of black money and black wealth, such as foreign assets and real estate would be appropriate. The target for tracking black money in the form of gold should be focused on traders in jewellery.

What Next?

In mid-February 2017, three months after Prime Minister Narendra Modi's announcement on demonetisation, there were no immediate gains to be seen from the decision. True, the benefits, if any, of something as major as Demonetisation 2016 cannot be reaped immediately, they are to be had only in the long term. There was one immediate outcome and this was the colossal amount of hardship experienced by the citizens of India. That most of the affected people did not openly express their unhappiness at having to bear this hardship does not reduce its severity.

While many economists forecast that the Indian economy had experienced significant damage from which recovery would be slow, some said that the economy would quickly bounce back from the downturn in growth. As of mid-February, there was no evidence of that as yet, but even if that happened, why cause a dislocation in the first place?

All the disruption and distress, to what purpose? When assessed in terms of the objectives of Demonetisation 2016, the outcome was unclear.

The government is yet (mid-February 2017) to present an estimate of how much of counterfeit currency that had been in circulation had been neutralised by demonetisation. It would also be time before the efficacy of the new security features in defeating counterfeiting could be assessed. In any case, as has been argued in this book, dealing with counterfeit currency did not require the suddenness and consequent harshness of a design and implementation as contained in Demonetisation 2016.

Originally, the main objective was to destroy black money held as cash in the form of Rs 500 and Rs 1,000 notes. But it is in the unearthing of black money that the outcome of Demonetisation 2016 has been very clearly limited. Demonetisation has not, as promised, turned 'worthless' the black money held in high denomination notes. The numbers released until early December 2016 indicated that most of the currency had already entered the banking system. Very little seemed to have been held back by holders of black money scared to enter the banking system.

The success of Demonetisation 2016 in unearthing black money that was circulating in the form of the demonetised high denomination notes now depends, in the first instance, on the new amnesty scheme, the PMGKY, receiving a large amount of disclosures. If the PMGKY does not yield declarations running into lakhs of crores (trillions) of rupees, yet another avenue will have to be explored. That would be the income tax authorities identifying holders of black money who did not take advantage of the PMGKY. Will the government, keen to show it has been successful with the demonetisation exercise, ask the income tax authorities to go after all those who made large deposits in banks between 10 November and 30 December 2016? This raises the spectre of harassment. Indeed the biggest concern, irrespective of the assurances of the government, is that we are now entering an era of tax harassment as government agencies set about trying to prove that Demonetisation 2016 was a major success in unearthing black money and improving tax compliance.

One of the central arguments in this book is that whichever way one looks at it, Demonetisation 2016 was not a good idea. One, very little of black money is held in the form of cash, so demonetisation was not going to destroy much of the unaccounted wealth. Two, even if the government did want to track down unaccounted cash, demonetisation itself was not the best way to go about it since it hurt the entire population while trying to ensnare a small number of holders of illicit cash. An alternative would have been to collect, analyse and follow up on information on large cash withdrawals from banks and thereby identify possible flows of unaccounted cash. Three, if, in spite of all the risks and limited chances of success, the government still wanted to go ahead with demonetisation, then the manner in which Demonetisation 2016 was designed and implemented was neither the only option nor the best one. There were other less destructive options available.

In public discussion, 'formalisation of the informal' emerged as a new rationale for Demonetisation 2016 after the event. Demonetisation and then digitalisation of monetary transactions would compel, it was argued, the informal sector to be henceforth more tax compliant. It was also argued that the introduction of the Goods and Services Tax (GST) would only strengthen this process. It is indeed well-known that in large sections of the informal sector—real estate, retail and wholesale trade, and professional services—payment of taxes is often not the norm. Demonetisation and digitalisation may drag these economic agents into the formal sector and lead to greater tax compliance. However, the fundamental problem with the 'formalisation of the informal' argument is that the much larger informal sector that ekes out its livelihood on the margins does not avoid paying taxes, it just earns too little to fall into the tax bracket. Formalisation of production by the tiny enterprises in industry, road-side service establishments, and by small- and medium-sized farmers would not lead to a gain to society. It would, in fact, put an additional burden on these producers who are already struggling by earning low incomes.

Some weeks after demonetisation was announced and when it became clear that a large amount of the high denomination notes had already entered the banking system, digitalisation emerged as the main agenda from Demonetisation 2016. It remains the most important item on the agenda. The focus now is on how to accelerate the adoption of electronic payments at all levels—from households upwards. There remain many infrastructural and economic constraints to accelerating digitalisation. That, however, is not the issue with the emergence of digitalisation as an action programme after Demonetisation 2016. The main issue is, did the economy have to be put through the demonetisation wringer in order to drive it towards digitalisation?

Digitalisation of payments is a process that has been underway in India for a decade and more. It has made considerable progress in transactions between companies in the organised sector and among those comfortable with electronic/on-line forms of payment. The larger population is, however, right now outside the scope of digital payments. Even with the Jan Dhan financial inclusion programme and the telecom revolution, major constraints in infrastructure and also issues relating to a lack of familiarity and unaffordability tell us that digitalisation cannot be hurried without running the risk of exclusion. Yet, the one major agenda that the government has been driving since Demonetisation 2016 has been digitalisation.

For some, it is not any concrete gain that matters, but the long-term 'psychological shock' that Demonetisation 2016 will inflict on the behaviour of people. The holders of black money will have experienced such a major shock that they will, it is said, decide that tax compliance is a better strategy than running the risk of losing everything in the future. But the immediate outcome seemed very much the opposite. That almost the entire stock of demonetised currency had entered the banking system showed the ease with which such individuals and organisations could get the better of the system. It also reflects the confidence they have of subsequently managing the system, in case there are to be investigations in the future.

The more likely psychological shock was a harmful one. Some commentators pointed out that the upheaval caused by the removal of 86 per cent of the currency in circulation had unnerved ordinary people, the honest citizens. The trust they had reposed in the currency issued by the central bank and the government had been shaken. This is an unhealthy development in a modern economy.

Yet, the promise initially was of something else. Soon after demonetisation had been announced, in the intense debate that followed it was pointed out by many that this action by itself would do little to destroy black money and do even less to end the future generation of black money. The government in response said that demonetisation was neither the first nor the last measure to be taken to destroy black money. More steps were to follow in what was promised would be a larger war.

There was little of that kind to be seen in the next three months, save the limited measures on political party finance announced in the Union Budget for 2017–18. It appeared as if the promised action was not to follow.

There is, however, a great deal to be done if even a dent is to be made in India's black economy.

Here is an illustrative list of just a few things calling for administrative/legislative action, which is drawn from a comprehensive unpublished note titled 'Next Steps After Demonetisation'[1]:

- Appointment of the Lok Pal: Three years after the enactment of the Lok Pal and Lok Ayukta Act of 2013, the Lok Pal in which so much hope had earlier been placed to identify and punish the corrupt is yet to be appointed.

[1] V. Bhaskar, 2016, 'Next Steps After Demonetisation' December, mimeo.

- Rules prohibiting/punishing benami transactions: The Benami Transactions (Prohibition) Amendment Act, 2015 has been passed but the Act has not been notified and the rules have not been issued. The Act passed in 1988 had not been notified for 25 years. It was then amended, but it is yet to be operationalised.
- Tightening rules for punishment for bribery: The Prevention of Corruption (Amendment) Bill 2015 is yet to be passed. The bill proposes to tighten the rules in some respects, though it also weakens it in other areas.
- Citizens' right to public services: The Right of Citizens for Time Bound Delivery of Goods and Services and Redressal of their Grievances Bill, 2011 lapsed in 2011 and has not been re-introduced. The bill mandated the preparation of charters with time-lines for provision of certain public services and the citizen's right to complain against non-delivery. Another bill on the citizen's broader right to public services has been languishing in the draft stage since 2009. This is the Public Services (Protection and Regulation) Bill 2009.
- Transparency in government procurement: The Public Procurement Bill 2012, which has been in the draft stage, mandates transparency in central government procurement. It could, if implemented properly, reduce corruption in procurement.

This is only a brief list. There is much more to do in a number of other areas. For instance, as argued in this book, the interface between politics and business, which is a major source of black money generation, is crying out for an effective elimination of conflict of interest.

There is also the issue of malpractices in financial sector transactions which are a major source of generation of black money.

Indeed, while the government was going after black money held as cash, less was said about the illegal transactions that take place in the financial sector, which are recorded in the banking sector and yet escape the gaze of the income tax authorities. Government committees have in the past highlighted the growth in transactions such as over/under invoicing of trade, share price manipulation through shell companies, round-tripping of capital through participatory notes, flows to tax havens, etc. It has been argued in this book that the generation of illicit income via such transactions conducted through the banking sector (with each transaction being large in value) may now be as much if not more than what is created and held in the form of cash.

A striking contemporary example of how undocumented money flows through the banking system is that which was brought out in the disproportionate assets trial of J. Jayalalithaa, when she was Chief Minister of Tamil Nadu, and her associate V. K. Sasikala. Thirty-four shell companies operating 50 bank accounts were used to illegally acquire/sell property and conduct other illicit transactions. This happened more than two decades ago. It boggles the mind to imagine the sophistication of illegal financial transactions that has since developed. A beginning has been reported to have been made in cracking down on shell companies, but the task of dismantling illegal transactions in the financial sector is no simple challenge.

Doing away with black money goes beyond taking specific measures or enacting new pieces of legislation. All three arms of the state—the legislature, the executive and the judiciary—have allowed black money to become a part and parcel of the Indian economy and society.

But the generation of black money is not just an outcome of the undermining of legislation by public institutions.

Ending black money calls for a larger change in governance, practices, attitudes and habits. These are changes that must be made not merely in the arms of the state but also within larger society. It is now acceptable for business to operate the levers of political power to get things done. It is now acceptable for political parties and political agents to abuse their office for the smallest of gains to the biggest of pay-offs. It is now acceptable for professional associations to condone violations of the norms of professional behaviour. It is now acceptable for the more powerful of citizens to proudly state that they flout rules, possess wealth beyond their means, and evade payment of taxes. It matters nothing that they flaunt ill-gotten wealth.

Root and branch overhaul in the society is then required to defeat black money.

If in the end Demonetisation 2016 turns out to have been a failure and if there is no follow up action on black money, there is likely to be long-term damage. The colossal distress that Demonetisation 2016 caused will make it impossible for any future government to embark on a more serious war on black money. The government will be wary if there is even a small risk of pain being inflicted once again on the entire population. No society will be able to go through this suffering once again. The black economy will then remain in place.

Bibliography

Demonetisation 2016: An Unfolding Story

Ahluwalia, Montek. 2016. 'Demonetisation: The Good, the Bad and the Ugly', *Mint*, 25 November, available at http://www.livemint.com/Opinion/cA5tkx4L7E1MMkP8quR6xJ/Demonetisation-The-good-the-bad-and-the-ugly.html, accessed on 4 December 2016.

Basu, Kaushik. 2016. 'Demonetization Will Put Only a Temporary Dent in Corruption, If Even That, and It May Rock the Entire Economy', *New York Times*, 27 November, available at https://www.nytimes.com/2016/11/27/opinion/in-india-black-money-makes-for-bad-policy.html, accessed on 26 January 2017.

Bhagwati, Jagdish, Pravin Krishna and Suresh Sundaresan. 2016. 'War on Black Money: Demonetisation is a Courageous Reform That Will Bring Substantive Benefits', *The Times of India*, 13 December, available at http://blogs.timesofindia.indiatimes.com/toi-edit-page/war-on-black-money-demonetisation-is-a-courageous-reform-that-will-bring-substantive-benefits/, accessed on 10 January 2017.

Chishti, Seema. 2016. 'Interview: Demonetisation Move Declares All Indians as Possible Crooks, Unless They Can Establish Otherwise, Says Amartya Sen', *The Indian Express*, 26 November, available at http://indianexpress.com/article/india/india-news-india/interview-move-declares-all-indians-as-possible-crooks-unless-they-can-establish-otherwise-says-amartya-sen/, accessed on 12 February 2017.

Dasgupta, Dipankar. 2016. 'Theoretical Analysis of Demonetisation', *Economic and Political Weekly*, 16 December, available at http://www.epw.in/journal/2016/51/notes/theoretical-analysis-%E2%80%98demonetisation%E2%80%99.html, accessed on 30 December 2016.

Ghosh, Jayati. 2016. 'Money and Social Contract', *Frontline*, 23 December, available at http://www.frontline.in/cover-story/money-and-social-contract/article9415055.ece, accessed 12 February 2017.

GoI (Government of India). 2017a. *Economic Survey 2016–17*, New Delhi: Ministry of Finance.

———. 2017b. *Union Budget 2017–18*, New Delhi: Ministry of Finance.

Iyer, Vaidyanathan P. 2016. 'Arvind Panagariya Raises First Red Flag on Tax Harassment', *The Indian Express*, 2 January, available at http://indianexpress.com/article/india/arvind-panagariya-raises-first-red-flag-on-tax-harassment-4455006/, accessed on 4 January 2017.

Jackson Institute of Global Affairs. 2016. 'Trump's Win and Modi's Demonetization: Challenges for Central Banks Around the World', Informal discussion with Rakesh Mohan, 6 December, mimeo.

Joseph, Tony. 2016. 'The Real Reasons for Demonetisation Might be Hiding in Plain Sight', *The Indian Express,* 19 December, available at http://indianexpress.com/article/blogs/demonetisation-implementation-cash-crunch-digital-payments-cashless-transactions-4435312/, accessed on 12 February 2017.

Kazmin, Amy. 2016. 'India: Narendra Modi's Bonfire of the Rupees', *Financial Times,* 17 November, available at https://www.ft.com/content/0467b734-ac23-11e6-ba7d-76378e4fef24, accessed on 26 November 2016.

Kelkar, Vijay, and Ajay Shah. 2016. 'Six Battlefronts for the War on Corruption', *Mint*, 21 November, available at http://www.livemint.com/Opinion/d7V9V6xUulbGWr5LLjttDJ/Six-battlefronts-for-the-war-on-corruption.html, accessed on 21 November 2016.

Kerala State Planning Board. 2016. *Interim Report of the Committee to Study the Impact of Demonetisation on the State Economy of Kerala*, December, Government of Kerala.

Krishnan, Ravi. 2017. 'Demonetisation is a Major Assault on Poor: Economist Pranab Bardhan', available at http://www.livemint.com/Politics/mR5PjTnEWfgQdOXKk3bZiL/Demonetisation-is-a-major-assault-on-poor-Economist-Pranab.html, *Mint 14 January,* accessed on 24 January 2017.

Mehta, Pratap Bhanu. 2016. 'It's Permanent Revolution', *The Indian Express*, 26 November, available at http://indianexpress.com/article/opinion/columns/demonetisation-currency-rs-5001000-notes-ban-demonetisation-effects-debate-its-permanent-revolution-4395371/, accessed on 28 November 2016.

Mody, Ashoka, and Michael Walton. 2017. 'Note Ban and the Allure of Authoritarian Populism', *Business Standard*, 10 January, available at http://www.business-standard.com/article/opinion/note-ban-and-the-allure-of-authoritarian-populism-117011001493_1.html, accessed on 11 January 2017.

Panagariya, Arvind. 2016. 'Economic Logic behind Demonetisation: Interview'. *India Today.in*, 1 December, available at https://www.youtube.com/watch?v=8tY4Ih8B88g&ab_channel=IndiaToday, accessed on 14 December 2016.

Patnaik, Prabhat. 2016. 'The Demonetization Fiasco', IDEAs, 16 January, available at http://www.networkideas.org/whats-new/2017/01/the-demonetization-fiasco/, accessed on 12 February 2017.

Rai, Suyash. 2016. 'The Demonetisation Decision: Event, Impact, Narrative and Meaning', *The Wire*, 4 December, available at http://thewire.in/84328/demonetisation-costs-benefits-analysis/, accessed on 5 December 2016.

Rangarajan, C. 2016. 'Make the Most Out of Demonetisation', *BusinessLine*, 14 November, avialbel at http://www.thehindubusinessline.com/opinion/demonetisation-black-money-and-reforms/article9349738.ece, accessed on 12 February 2017.

Rao, Govinda M. 2016. 'Demonetisation: Is the Pain Commensurate with Gain?' Text of lecture delivered at Centre for Multi-Disciplinary Research, Dharwad, Karnataka on 8 December 2016. Reprinted as Takshashila Essay December 2016.

Rogoff, Kenneth. 2016. 'India's Cash Bonfire is Too Much, Too Soon', *Financial Times*, 9 December, available at https://www.ft.com/content/59c3e922-bd72-11e6-8b45-b8b81dd5d080, accessed on 15 December 2016.

Sharma, Ruchir. 2016. 'Revenge No Development Strategy: Populist Nationalism Cannot Paper over Economic Chaos Unleashed by Demonetisation Drive', *The Times of India*, 21 November, available on http://blogs.timesofindia.indiatimes.com/toi-edit-page/revenge-no-development-strategy-populist-nationalism-cannot-paper-over-economic-chaos-unleashed-by-demonetisation-drive/, accessed on 22 November 2016.

Srivasatava, Sanjay. 2016. 'For India's Middle Classes, Demonetisation Has Become a Moral Project', *Scroll.in*, available at http://scroll.in/article/821478/demonetisation-lacks-economic-logic-but-for-indias-middle-classes-its-now-a-moral-project, accessed on 14 December 2016.

Subbarao, Duvurri. 2016. 'Demonetisation—Is This Time Different?', ISAS Insights Number 363, 14 November, Institute of South Asian Studies, Singapore.

The Economist. 2016a. 'India's Currency Reform was Botched in Execution', 3 December, available at http://www.economist.com/news/leaders/21711040-narendra-modi-needs-take-measures-mitigate-damage-his-rupee-reform-has-done-indias, accessed on 14 December 2016.

———. 2016b. 'Modi's Attempt to Crush the Black Economy is Hurting the Poor', 3 December, available at http://www.economist.com/news/asia/21711094-without-cash-indians-are-struggling-modis-attempt-crush-black-economy-hurting-poor, accessed on 4 December 2016.

The Indian Express. 2016. 'Both Sides of the Coin: What Top Economists Think about Demonetisation', 28 November, available at http://indianexpress.com/article/india/india-news-india/both-sides-of-the-coin-what-top-economists-think-about-demonetisation/, accessed on 29 November 2016.

Thorat, Usha. 2016. 'A Note to RBI', *The Indian Express*, 28 December, available at http://indianexpress.com/article/opinion/columns/reserve-bank-of-india-rbi-remonetisation-rules-problems-note-to-bank-4447698/, accessed on 10 January 2017.

Venugopal, Vasudha. 2016. 'Demonetisation in a Booming Economy is Like Shooting at the Tyres of a Racing Car: Jean Drèze', *Economic Times*, 22 November, available at http://economictimes.indiatimes.com/opinion/interviews/demonetisation-in-a-booming-economy-is-like-shooting-at-the-tyres-of-a-racing-car-jean-drze/articleshow/55547554.cms, accessed on 22 November 2016.

Chapter 1

Business Standard Web Team. 'What is Benami Property: All Your Questions Answered', *Business Standard*, 14 November, available at http://www.business-standard.com/article/current-affairs/what-is-benami-property-all-your-questions-answered-116111400263_1.html, accessed on 1 December 2016.

Ministry of Finance. 2012. 'Black Money: White Paper', New Delhi, May 2012.

_____. 2012. 'Measures to Tackle Black Money in India and Abroad: Report of the Committee headed by Chairman CBDT', parts I and II. New Delhi: Government of India.

Reddy, Y. V. 2016. 'Understanding Black Money in India', Second Mahesh Buch Lecture delivered in Bhopal on 5 October.

CHAPTER 2

Ministry of Finance. 2012. 'Black Money: White Paper', New Delhi, May 2012.

The Hindu, The Black Economy Now Amounts to 75% of GDP', available at http://www.thehindu.com/news/national/black-economy-now-amounts-to-75-of-gdp/article6278286.ece, accessed on 19 December 2016.

CHAPTER 3

Edelbacher, Maximilian, Peter C. Kratcoski and Bojan Dobovšek, ed. 2016. *Corruption, Fraud, Organized Crime, and the Shadow Economy.* Boca Raton: CRC Press: Taylor and Francis.

Lippert, Owen, and David Walker. 1997. *The Underground Economy: Global Evidence of Its Size and Impact*. Vancouver: Fraser Institute.

Schneider, Friedrich. 2006. 'Shadow Economies and Corruption All Over the World: What Do We Really Know?' Discussion Paper 2315, Institute for the Study of Labour, Bonn, Germany.

Schneider, Friederich, Andreas Buehn, and Claudio E. Montenegro. 2010. 'Shadow Economies All Over the World: New Estimates for 162 Countries from 1999 to 2007', World Bank, Policy Research Working Paper, Policy Research Working Paper 5356.

Schneider, Friedrich, and Dominik H. Enste. 2013. *The Shadow Economy: An International Survey*, second edition. New York: Cambridge University Press.

Singh, Anoop, Sonali Jain-Chandra, and Adil Mohommad. 2012. *Inclusive Growth, Institutions, and the Underground Economy*. IMF Working Paper.

Yikona, Stuart, Brigitte Slot, Michael Geller, Bjarne Hansen, and Fatima el Kadiri. 2011. *Il-Gotten Money and the Economy: Experiences from Malawi and Namibia*. Washington: World Bank.

CHAPTER 4

Oxford University Press. *Oxford Dictionaries Online*, available at https://www.oxforddictionaries.com/, accessed on 19 December 2016.

RBI (Reserve Bank of India). 1970. *History of the Reserve Bank of India*, volume 1 (1935–1951). Reprinted in 2005. Mumbai: RBI, available at https://rbidocs.rbi.org.in/rdocs/content/PDFs/89630.pdf, accessed on 19 December 2016.

——. 2005. *The Reserve Bank of India*, volume 3 (1967–1981). Mumbai: RBI, available at https://rbidocs.rbi.org.in/rdocs/content/PDFs/90060.pdf, accessed on 19 December 2016.

Reserve Bank of Zimbabwe. 2015. 'Demonetisation of the Zimbabwe Dollar', Press Statement, 15 June.

Varma, Sonal. 2016. 'India: Angels and Demonetisation'. *Nomura Asia Insights*, 11 November.

CHAPTER 5

BJP (Bharatiya Janata Party). 2014. 'Manifesto 2014', available at http://www.bjp.org/images/pdf_2014/full_manifesto_english_07.04.2014.pdf, accessed on 20 December 2016.

Congress Party. 2014. 'Manifesto 2014', available at http://inc.in/images/pages/English%20Manifesto%20for%20Web.pdf, accessed on 20 December 2016.

PIB (Press Information Bureau). 2016a. 'India and Mauritius Sign the Protocol for Amendment of the Convention', 10 May.

——. 2016b. 'Government Takes Various Steps in Last Two Years to Curb the Menace of Black Money both Within and Outside the Country', 10 May.

——. 2016c. 'Prohibition of Benami Property Transactions Act, 1988', press release, 16 October.

PRS. 2015a. 'Bill Summary: The Black Money (Undisclosed Foreign Income and Assets) and Imposition of Tax Act', 20 April, available at http://www.prsindia.org/uploads/media/Black%20Money/Bill%20

Summary%20--%20Undisclosed%20Foreign%20Income.pdf, accessed on 20 December 2016.

______. 2015b. 'Bill Summary: The Benami Transactions (Prohibition) Amendment Bill, 2015', 29 May, available at http://www.prsindia.org/uploads/media/Benami/Bill%20Summary-%20Benami%20Transactions.pdf, accessed on 20 December 2016.

Supreme Court of India. 2011. *'Ram Jethmalani & Ors vs Union of India & Ors'*, on 4 July, available at https://indiankanoon.org/doc/1232445/, accessed on 20 December 2016.

The Indian Express. 2016. 'PM Modi Steps In', 5 April, available at http://indianexpress.com/article/india/india-news-india/panama-papers-pm-modi-has-asked-to-probe-the-matter-says-arun-jaitley/, accessed on 20 December 2016.

CHAPTER 6

Ministry of Finance. 2012. 'Black Money: White Paper', New Delhi, May 2012.

CHAPTER 7

Ashok, Krithika. 2016. 'Demonetisation: Can the State Legally Deprive People of Their Own Money?' *Business Standard*, December 5.

Chidambaram, P. 2016. 'Monumental Mismanagement', 4 December, available at http://pchidambaram.in/across-the-aisle-monumental-mismanagement/, accessed on 28 January 2017.

Kumar, Alok Prasanna. 2016. 'Demonetisation and the Rule of Law'. *Economic and Political Weekly* 51 (50), 10 December.

Ministry of Finance. 2012. 'Measures to Tackle Black Money in India and Abroad'. *Report of the Committee Headed by Chairman CBDT, parts I and II*. New Delhi: Government of India.

Nag, Ashok. 2016. 'Lost Due to Demonetisation'. *Economic and Political Weekly* 51 (48), 26 November.

Rajakumar, Dennis J., and S. L. Shetty. 2016. 'Demonetisation: 1978, Present and the Aftermath', *Economic and Political Weekly*, 26 November, available at http://www.epw.in/journal/2016/48/commentary/demonetisation-1978-present-and-aftermath.html, accessed on 10 December 2016.

Rath, Nilakantha. 2016. 'Measuring Narendra Modi's Monumental Mismanagement', *Mint*, 23 December, available at http://www.livemint.com/Opinion/DFsK242FGYdYYTCSr35d8H/Measuring-Narendra-Modis-monumental-mismanagement.html, accessed on 25 December 2016.

Reserve Bank of India. 2016. *Report of the Reserve Bank of India 2015–16*. Mumbai: RBI.

Yadav, Yogendra. 2017. 'The Devil is in the Fine Print', *The Hindu*, 16 February, available at http://www.thehindu.com/opinion/lead/The-devil-is-in-the-fine-print/article17308089.ece, accessed on 17 February.

Chapter 8

Banerjee, Subhashis. 2016. 'There is No Magical Switch That Will Allow India to Go Cashless', *The Wire*, 15 December, available at http://thewire.in/86893/no-off-switch-will-allow-india-magically-migrate-cashless-economy/, accessed on 22 December 2016.

Chakravorti, Bhaskar. 2016. 'India's Botched War on Cash', *Harvard Business Review*, available at https://hbr.org/2016/12/indias-botched-war-on-cash, accessed on 20 December 2016.

Committee for Digital Payments. 2016. 'Medium Term Recommendations to Strengthen the Digital Payment Ecosystem', Ministry of Finance, December.

Demirguc-Kunt, Asli. 2015. 'The Global Findex Database 2014 Measuring Financial Inclusion Around the World'. *World Bank Working Paper* 2755. Geneva: The World Bank.

Department of Economic Affairs. 2016. 'Promotion of Payments Through Cards and Digital Means', Ministry of Finance, Office Memorandum 29 February, available at http://dea.gov.in/sites/default/files/Promo_PaymentsMeans_Card_Digital_0.pdf, accessed on 4 December 2016

Drèze, Jean. 2015. 'JAM and the Pursuit of Nirvana'. *The Wire*, 6 November 2015, available at http://thewire.in/14873/jam-and-the-pursuit-of-nirvana/, accessed on 10 January 2017

Economic Survey 2014–15. 2015. 'Wiping Every Tear from Every Eye: The JAM Number Trinity Solution', chapter 3.

First Post. 2016. 'Demonetisation: How Narendra Modi Changed Narrative from Black Money to Cashless Economy', available at http://www.firstpost.com/politics/note-ban-how-narendra-modi-changed-narrative-from-black-money-to-cashless-economy-3127628.html, accessed on 23 January 2016.

Joseph, Nikhil, Ruben Korenke, Benjamin D. Mazzotta, and Bhaskar Chakravorti. 2013. 'India Cash Outlook' IBGC Working Paper 13-01, The Fletcher School, Tuft University.

NDTV. 2016. *Note Ban Shock Is Good For India: Nandan Nilekani To NDTV*, available at https://www.youtube.com/watch?v=aQL2OSLKtp0&ab_channel=NDTV, accessed on 9 December.

Pahwa, Nikhil. 2016. 'Cash vs Digital Money: Why Going Cashless Is Going to Be Tough in India'. *MediaNama*, 29 November, available at http://www.medianama.com/2016/11/223-cashless-india/, accessed on 9 February 2017.

PMJDY (Pradhan Mantri Jan Dhan Yojana). 2016. 'Progress Report', available at http://www.pmjdy.gov.in/account, accessed on 9 December 2016.

PWC (PricewaterhouseCoopers). 2014. 'Disrupting Cash: Accelerating Electronic Payments in India', available at https://www.pwc.in/.../disrupting-cash-accelerating-electronic-payments-in-india.pd, accessed on 9 February 2017.

Reserve Bank of India (RBI). 2016a. *Payment and Settlement Systems in India Vision 2018*. Mumbai: RBI.

RBI. 2016b. 'Concept Paper on Card Infrastructure. Mumbai: RBI.

———. 2015. *Report of the Committee on Medium-term Path on Financial Inclusion*. Mumbai: RBI.

Shrivastava, Prachi. 2016. 'Privacy Not a Fundamental Right, Argues Mukul Rohatgi for Govt as Govt Affidavit Says Otherwise', available at http://www.legallyindia.com/Constitutional-law/privacy-not-a-fundamental-right-argues-mukul-rohatgi-for-govt-as-govt-affidavit-says-otherwise, accessed on 8 December.

TiE Bangalore. 2015. *Disruption in Financial Services: Nandan Nilekani at TiE LeapFrog*, available at https://www.youtube.com/watch?v=aGM5TvAUF00&ab_channel=TiEBangalore, accessed on 9 December.

Thomas, Hugh. 2013. 'Measuring Progress Towards a Cashless Society', available at http://www.mastercardadvisors.com/_assets/pdf/MasterCardAdvisors-CashlessSociety.pdf, accessed on December 15 2016.

TRAI (Telecom Regulatory Authority of India). 2016a. 'The Indian Telecom Services Performance Indicators'. January-March, 5 August.

TRAI. 2016b. 'Highlights of Telecom Subscription Data as on 31st July, 2016', Press Release 7 October, 2016.

Visa. 2016. *Accelerating the Growth of Digital Payments in India: A Five-Year Outlook.*

CHAPTER 9

I. Sources for Table 9.1

Asian Development Outlook 2016: Asia's Growth Potential, Asian Development Bank, 13 December 2016, available at https://www.adb.org/sites/default/files/publication/182221/ado2016.pdf.

Bhargava, Deepali. 2016.'India: The J-curve impact of demonetization', *Emerging Markets Quaterly: Q1 2017* (exact excerpt), Credit Suisse, 16 December 2016; 'Asia Insights', available at https://doc.research-and-analytics.csfb.com/docView?language=ENG&format=PDF&sourceid=em&document_id=1068295791&serialid=ZqC5OSiikM6eEXX3FM4ZUkd5QqIosfUMLBBxxdt7EcY%3D, accessed on 1 February 2017.

'Economy Insights', *Ambit Capital*, 18 November 2016, available at http://reports.ambitcapital.com/reports/Ambit_Economy_Insight_MRTresetstothefore_18Nov2016.pdf; 'Economy Insights', *Ambit Capital*, 21 December 2016, available at http://reports.ambitcapital.com/reports/Ambit_Economy_Insight_Aneconomichammeringisagiven_21Dec2016.pdf, accessed on 1 February 2017.

Fifth Bi-monthly Monetary Policy Statement, 2016–17 Resolution of the Monetary Policy Committee (MPC), Reserve Bank of India, 7 December 2016, available at https://www.rbi.org.in/Scripts/BS_PressReleaseDisplay.aspx?prid=38818, accessed on 1 February 2017.

Fitch on India—Bi-Monthly Newsletter, Fitch Ratings, available at https://www.fitchratings.com/site/re/892519, accessed on 1 February 2017

'Impact of Demonetization on GDP Growth in FY17', Care Ratings, 18 November, http://www.careratings.com/upload/NewsFiles/Economics/Impact%20of%20demonetization%20on%20GDP.pdf, accessed on 1 February 2017.

'Indian Economy', ICRA Ratings, December 2016, http://www.icra.in/Files/Articles/ICRA%20Macro%20Update%20December%202016.pdf, accessed on 1 February 2017.

'India's Real GDP Growth to Slip to 6% in 2016–17: Demonetisation to Cause Sustained Downturn', by Mahesh Vyas, Centre for Monitoring

Indian Economy, Economic Outlook, 12 January 2017, available at https://www.cmie.com/kommon/bin/sr.php?kall=warticle&dt=2017-01-12%2017:49:49&msec=646, accessed on 1 February 2017.

Mishra, Asit Ranjan. 2016. 'Demonetisation Fallout: ADB Reduces India GDP Growth Forecast to 7%', *LiveMint*, 14 December 2016, available at http://www.livemint.com/Politics/Vz3abbBkVLzpUgZK71FbVM/Demonetisation-fallout-ADB-reduces-Indias-growth-forecast.html, accessed on 1 February 2017.

Press Note on First Advance Estimates of National Income 2016–17, Central Statistics Office, Ministry of Statistics and Programme Implementation, Government of India, available at http://pib.nic.in/newsite/PrintRelease.aspx?relid=156182, accessed on 1 February 2017.

World Bank. *World Economic Prospects: Weak Investment in Uncertain Times,* World Bank, January 2017, available at https://openknowledge.worldbank.org/bitstream/handle/10986/25823/9781464810169.pdf,accessed on 1 February 2017.

World Economic Outlook Update, 16 January 2017, International Monetary Fund, available at https://www.imf.org/external/pubs/ft/weo/2017/update/01/pdf/0117.pdf, accessed on 1 February 2017.

II. Special Reports and Series

Business Standard. 2016. 'Caught in the Spiral' Series on Cottage Industries: Dharavi, 19 December, Bhiwandi, 20 December, Sivakasi, 21 December, Assam Tea Gardens, 23 December, and Solapur, 24–25 December.

_____. 2016. 'Demonetisation: Trade Blues—Indore', 29 December, available at http://www.business-standard.com/article/economy-policy/sarafa-bazar-loses-its-glitter-116112900019_1.html, accessed on 1 December 2016, Series on Trade in Six Cities.

Frontline. 2016. 'Monumental Blunder', 6 December, available at http://www.frontline.in/magazine/?date=2016-12-06&magid=9374246, accessed on 30 January 2017.

India Today. 2016. 'Havoc in the Hinterland', available at http://indiatoday.intoday.in/story/demonetisation-rural-distress-choked-currency-flow/1/823790.html, accessed on 6 December 2016.

III. Articles and Reports

Anand, Geeta, and Hari Kumar. 2017. 'In Its Third Month, India's Cash Shortage Begins to Bite', *New York Times*, 24 January, available at https://www.nytimes.com/2017/01/24/world/asia/in-its-third-month-indias-cash-shortage-begins-to-bite.html?_r=0, accessed on 26 January.

Apoorva. 2016, 'Uttar Pradesh-Bihar Border Refrain: Will Wait 20 More Days, After That....' *The Indian Express*, 8 December, available at http://indianexpress.com/article/india/uttar-pradesh-bihar-border-demonetisation-impact-cash-crunch-cashless-economy-note-ban-4416068/, accessed on 26 January 2016.

Basu, Kaushik. 2016. 'Demonetization Will Put Only a Temporary Dent in Corruption, If Even That, and It May Rock the Entire Economy', *New York Times*, 27 November, available at https://www.nytimes.com/2016/11/27/opinion/in-india-black-money-makes-for-bad-policy.html, accessed on 26 January 2017.

Bera, Sayantan. 2016. 'Farm Incomes Dented as Note ban Drives Down Prices of Perishables' *Mint*, 20 December.

Bhattacharya, Amit, and Subodh Varma. 2016. 'Note Ban: Trade Slows to a Trickle at MP Mandi's Busiest Time of Year', *The Times of India*, 10 January 2017, available at http://epaperbeta.timesofindia.com/Article.aspx?eid=31808&articlexml=NOTES-FROM-THE-GROUND-Two-months-on-rural-11012017011028, accessed on 24 January 2017.

Bhowmik, Sharmila. 2016. 40% Layoff of Contract Workers in Noida Units in 40 Days of Demonetisation, *The Times of India*, 20 December, available at http://timesofindia.indiatimes.com/city/noida/40-layoff-of-contract-workers-in-noida-units-in-40-days-of-demonetisation/articleshow/56087069.cms, accessed on 27 January 2017.

Business Standard. 2017. 'Warning Signals', Editorial, available at http://www.business-standard.com/article/opinion/warning-signals-117012401448_1.html, accessed on 26 January 2017.

Catchnews. 2016. 'From Barter to Credit: This is How Rural India Coping with the Demonetisation Cash Crunch', 6 December, available at www.catchnews.com/india-news/from-barter-to-credit-this-is-how-rural-india-coping-with-the-demonetisation-cash-crunch-1479478607.html, accessed on 6 December 2016.

Das, Sohni, and Vimukt Dave. 2016. 'Demonetisation Impact: Migrant Workers Head Back Home', *Business Standard*, 10 December, available at http://www.business-standard.com/article/economy-policy/demonetisation-impact-migrant-workers-head-back-home-116120901022_1.html, accessed on 30 January 2017.

Dasgupta, Manas. 2016. 'Barter System Comes to Gujaratis' Aid', *The Tribune*, 5 December, available at http://www.tribuneindia.com/news/nation/barter-system-comes-to-gujaratis-aid/332550.html, accessed on 6 December 2016.

Dey, Abhishek. 2016. 'A Morning Spent in a Queue to Withdraw Cash is a Day Without Earning a Wage, Say Factory Workers', *Scroll.in*, 2 December, available at https://scroll.in/article/823037/a-morning-spent-in-a-queue-to-withdraw-cash-is-a-day-without-earning-a-wage-say-factory-workers, accessed on 30 January 2017.

Dreze, Jean, Dheeraj Kumar and Akash Ranjan. 2016. 'Demonetisation Decimates Ranchi's Economy', 26 December, available at https://thewire.in/89498/demonetisation-decimates-ranchis-economy/, accessed on 30 December 2016.

IIIFL. 2016. 'Demonetisation—Rural Visit: No V-Shaped Recovery', Indiainfoline, Mimeo: 8 December.

Jain, Mayank. 2016. 'Helpless And Cashless in Thane: Workers Suffer As Businesses Struggle on Pay Day', *Quint*, 1 December, available at http://www.bloombergquint.com//business/2016/12/01/helpless-and-cashless-in-thane-workers-suffer-as-businesses-struggle-on-pay-day, accessed on 10 December 2017.

Jaiswal, Anuja, and Arvind Chauhan. 2016. 'In Times of Notebandi, Nasbandi Rises', *The Times of India*, 27 November.

Jamir, Moa. 2016. 'Transport Stumbles, Villagers Confused: Nagaland Struggles with Demonetisation', *Scroll.in,* available at http://scroll.in/article/821549/no-cash-in-atms-transport-hit-villagers-confused-nagaland-struggles-with-demonetisation, accessed on 1 December 2016.

Jha, Nishita. 2016. 'What of the Women Who Hide Cash to Feed Their Children or to Escape Abuse?' 12 November, *Scroll.in*, available at http://scroll.in/article/821255/note-demonetisation-what-of-the-women-who-hide-cash-to-feed-their-children-or-to-escape-abuse, accessed on 14 November 2016.

Johari, Aarefa. 2016. 'From Wholesalers to Daily-Wage Earners, Demonetisation Has Hurt All Indians Who Use Cash', *Scroll.in*, available at http://scroll.in/article/821424/from-wholesalers-to-labourers-on-the-margins-demonetisation-has-hit-everyone-in-the-cash-economy, accessed on 1 December 2016.

Krishnan, Ravi. 2017. 'Demonetisation is a Major Assault on Poor: Economist Pranab Bardhan', available at http://www.livemint.com/Politics/mR5PjTnEWfgQdOXKk3bZiL/Demonetisation-is-a-major-assault-on-poor-Economist-Pranab.html, *Mint*, 14 January, accessed on 24 January 2017.

Kumar, Ashok. 2017. 'Note Ban Puts Brakes on Auto Jobs', *The Hindu*, 13 January, available at http://www.thehindu.com/news/cities/Delhi/Note-ban-puts-brakes-on-auto-jobs/article17031109.ece, accessed on 27 January 2017.

Lele, Abhijit, and Nupur Anand. 2016.'Demonetisation Impact: Money Lenders Make a Comeback', *Business Standard*, 26 December, available at http://www.business-standard.com/article/economy-policy/demonetisation-impact-money-lenders-make-a-comeback-116122601048_1.html, accessed on 30 January 2017.

Mahaprashasta, Ajoy Ashirwad. 2016. 'Demonetisation Has Broken Bundelkhand's Labour Migration Cycle', *The Wire*, 23 December, available at https://thewire.in/88971/bundelkhand-demonetisation-labour-migration/, accessed on 30 January 2017.

Makkar, Sahil. 2016. 'Demonetisation: Daily Wagers Fighting the Crisis by Skipping One Meal a Day', *The Economic Times*, 20 November, available at http://www.business-standard.com/article/economy-policy/demonetisation-daily-wagers-fighting-the-crisis-by-skipping-one-meal-a-day-116111900807_1.html, accessed on 30 January 2017.

Mander, Harsh, Anirban Bhattcharya, Nandini Dey and Vivek Mishra. 2017. 'Good for the Country, Not Good for the Poor: Delhi's Marginal Folk Struggle with Demonetisation', *Scroll.in*, available at https://scroll.in/article/823692/good-for-the-country-not-good-for-the-poor-delhis-marginal-folk-struggle-with-demonetisation, accessed on 31 January 2017.

Mitali, Nikore. 2016. 'Assessing the Impact of Demonetisation Through the Gender Lens', IGC, 20 December, available at https://www.theigc.org/blog/assessing-the-impact-of-demonetisation-through-the-gender-lens/, accessed on 26 January 2017.

Mukherjee, Sanjeeb. 2016. 'Rabi Sowing: Acreage More Than 2015, But Sowing Pace Slows Further, *Business Standard*, 26 November, available at http://www.business-standard.com/article/economy-policy/rabi-sowing-acreage-more-than-2015-but-sowing-pace-slows-further-116112501152_1.html, accessed on 25 January 2017.

Nanda, Prashant. 2016. 'Demonetisation: 35 Per Cent Job Losses, 50 Per Cent Revenue Dip, Says Study by Largest Organisation of Manufacturers', *Mint*, 25 November, available at http://www.livemint.com/Industry/JjUbakJtNbqo8sta5LQciL/Textile-hub-in-tatters-as-cash-crunch-takes-a-toll-on-produc.html, accessed on 26 January 2017.

Narayan, Sudha, and Nidhi Aggrawal. 2016. 'Demonetisation Alone Can't Turn Agricultural Markets Cashless', *The Wire*, 25 November, available at https://thewire.in/82485/demonetisation-agriculture-cashless-economy/, accessed on 26 December 2016.

NITI Aayog. 2017. 'Agricultural Growth in the Aftermath of Demonetization', available at http://niti.gov.in/content/agricultural-growth-aftermath-demonetization, accessed on 28 January 2017.

Pisharoty, Sangeeta Barooah. 2016. 'The Strange Effects of Demonetisation in the Northeast', *The Wire*, 18 November, available at https://thewire.in/81174/demonetisation-northeast-bhutan-newspapers/, accessed on 6 December 2016.

Roche, Elizabeth, and Prerna Kapoor. 2017. 'MGNREGS to See Record Spending as Demonetisation Drives Demand', *Mint*, 27 January, available at http://www.livemint.com/Politics/NltcLG5iMbkhm8v1tjrILO/MGNREGS-to-see-record-spending-as-demonetisation-raises-dema.html, accessed on 27 January 2017.

Saha, Devanik, and Swagata Yadavar. 2016. 'Demonetisation: Patients Face the Brunt as Private Hospitals Refuse to Take Old Notes', 28 November, available at http://www.thenewsminute.com/article/demonetisation-patients-face-brunt-private-hospitals-refuse-take-old-notes-53523, accessed on 26 January 2017.

Sally, Madhvi, and Jayashree Bhosale. 2016. 'Cheque Payments Making Farmers' Lives More Difficult', *The Economic Times*, 7 December, available at http://economictimes.indiatimes.com/news/economy/agriculture/cheque-payments-making-farmers-lives-more-difficult/articleshow/55843422.cms, accessed on 30 January 2017.

Sharma, Arun. 2017. 'Haroon and His Valley of Grief', *The Indian Express*, 17 January, available at http://indianexpress.com/article/india/haroon-and-his-valley-of-grief-4464186/, accessed on 17 February 2017.

Sharma, Nidhi. 2016. 'Farmers Suffer No Returns from Rich Harvest as Customers Have No Cash, *Economic Times*, 20 December, available at http://economictimes.indiatimes.com/news/politics-and-nation/farmers-suffer-no-returns-from-rich-harvest-as-customers-have-no-cash/articleshow/56073813.cms, accessed on 30 January 2017.

Sharma, Sahib. 2016. 'Cash-dominated Microfinance Sector Reels under Demonetization Stress', *Mint*, 18 November, available at http://www.livemint.com/Industry/CfB40Bu686ZaC6hk8isP7K/Cashdominated-microfinance-sector-reels-under-demonetizatio.html, accessed on 6 December 2016.

Singh, Ramendra, Maulshree Seth and Ishita Mishra. 2016. 'Demonetisation on a Shoestring: How UP Leather Industry is Hit by Cash Crunch', *The Indian Express*, 25 December, available at
http://indianexpress.com/article/india/demonetisation-on-a-shoestring-how-up-leather-industry-is-hit-by-cash-crunch-4443645/, accessed on 26 January 2017.

The Indian Express. 2016. 'Demonetisation: In Kutch Dust Bowl, Scrapped Notes Still Do the Rounds, 8 December, available at http://indianexpress.com/article/india/demonetisation-in-kutch-dust-bowl-scrapped-notes-still-do-the-rounds-4415890/, accessed on 6 December 2016.

———. 2016. 'Demonetisation Halts Disbursements by MFIs', 18 November, available at http://indianexpress.com/article/india/india-news-india/demonetisation-halts-disbursements-by-mfis-4383162/, accessed on 6 December 2016.

———. 2017. 'As Rural Hands Return, NREGA Demand Spikes Over 60 per cent 9 January', available at http://indianexpress.com/article/india/as-rural-hands-return-nrega-demand-spikes-over-60-per-cent-4465577/, accessed on 11 January 2017.

The Times of India. 2016. 'Maharashtra: Fishing Business Grinds to a Halt Due to Shortage of Cash, 6 December, available at http://timesofindia.indiatimes.com/city/kolhapur/Fishing-business-grinds-to-a-halt-due-to-shortage-of-cash/articleshow/55842158.cms, accessed on 30 January 2017.

_____. 2016. 'Gwalior Farmers Pay Kids' School Fees in Paddy', 25 December, available at http://timesofindia.indiatimes.com/city/bhopal/gwalior-farmers-pay-kids-school-fees-in-paddy/articleshow/56163293.cms?from=mdr, accessed on 11 January 2017.

_____. 2017. 'Two Months On, Rural Jobs in UP Still in Freeze Frame', 11 January, available at http://epaperbeta.timesofindia.com/Article.aspx?eid=31808&articlexml=NOTES-FROM-THE-GROUND-Two-months-on-rural-11012017011028, accessed on 26 January 2017.

Yadav, Anumeha, Mridula Chari and Abhishek Dey. 2017. 'Cashless and Demonetised: Meet Three Indians Who Once Had Jobs', *Scroll.in*, 29 January, available at https://scroll.in/article/827349/a-woman-construction-worker-in-jharkhand-lost-even-her-meagre-wages-in-10-weeks-since-demonetisation, accessed on 30 January 2017.

CHAPTER 10

ADR (Association for Democratic Reforms). 2017. 'Analysis of Sources of Funding of National and Regional Parties—FY 2004–05 to 2014–15', available at http://adrindia.org/content/analysis-sources-funding-national-and-regional-parties-fy-2004-05-2014-15-0, accessed on 29 January 2017.

_____. 2014. 'Circulation of Unaccounted Money in Activities Related to Electoral Process', ADR submission to SIT, 15 December, Annexure I, available at http://adrindia.org/content/circulation-unaccounted-money-activities-related-electoral-process-adr-submits-memorandum, accessed on 3 January 2017.

Bhaskar, V. 2016. 'Next Steps after Demonetisation', *Mimeo*, 26 December 2017.

Gowda, Rajeev M. V., and E. V. Sridharan, 2012. 'Reforming India's Party Financing and Election Expenditure Laws', *Election Law Journal*, volume 11, number 2.

Sastry, Trilochan. 2014. 'Towards Decriminalisation of Elections and Politics', *Economic Political Weekly* XLIX (1), 4 January 2014.

Sinha, Aseema. 2010. 'Business and Politics', in *Oxford Companion to Politics in India*. New Delhi: Oxford University Press.

The Hindu. 2013. 'Munde Admits Spending Rs 8 Crore in 2009 Polls', 28 June, available at http://www.thehindu.com/news/national/other-states/munde-admits-spending-rs-8-crore-in-2009-polls/article4857676.ece, accessed on 29 January.

Wade, Robert. 1985. 'The Market for Public Office: Why the Indian State is Not Better at Development', *World Development*, vol. 13, number 4.

Report of the Working Group to Study the Issues related to Gold Imports and Gold Loans NBFCs in India 2013, available at https://rbi.org.in/Scripts/PublicationReportDetails.aspx?ID=699, accessed on 9 February 2017.

Rediff.com. 2016. 'Will Modi Target Gold and Real Estate Next?', available at http://www.rediff.com/business/column/will-modi-target-gold-and-real-estate-next/20161212.htm, accessed on 23 January 2016.

The Financial Express. 2016. 'Gold in Your Lockers? Government Not to Tax Jewellery from Disclosed, Exempted Income', available at http://www.financialexpress.com/india-news/ancestral-jewellery-and-gold-not-chargeable-to-tax-under-amended-i-t-law-finance-ministry/461420/, accessed on 23 January 2016.

CHAPTER 11

IMF (International Monetary Fund). 2012. 'What is Money'. *Finance and Development* 49 (3), available at http://www.imf.org/external/pubs/ft/fandd/2012/09/basics.htm, accessed on 23 January 2017.

The Indian Express. 2016. 'An Overview of the Evolution of Paper Currency in India', available at http://indianexpress.com/article/research/demonetisation-five-hundred-one-thousand-rupees-500-1000-new-2000-rupees-an-overview-of-the-evolution-of-paper-currency-in-india-4378734/, accessed on 23 January 2017.

RBI (Reserve Bank of India). 2015. Reserve Bank of India *Annual Report 2015–16*. Mumbai: Reserve Bank of India.

CHAPTER 13

BIS (Bank of International Settlements). 2009. 'Issues in Governance of Central Banks', available at http://www.bis.org/publ/othp04.htm, accessed on 24 January 2017.

Reuters. 2016. 'S&P Says India's Demonetisation Hurts Confidence in RBI', 15 December, available at http://in.reuters.com/article/india-rbi-s-and-p-idINKBN14315V, accessed on 24 January 2017.

The Economist. 2016. 'The Ropy Rupee Recall: Modi's Attempt to Crush the Black Economy is Hurting the Poor', 3 December, available at http://www.economist.com/news/asia/21711094-without-cash-indians-are-struggling-modis-attempt-crush-black-economy-hurting-poor, accessed on 24 January 2017.

CHAPTER 14

Bernestein, Peter L. 2012. *The Power of Gold: The History of an Obsession*. Hoboken, NJ, United States: John Wiley and Sons.

First Post. 2016. 'Demonetisation: Nov Gold Imports at 100 t; Did Evaders Rush to Convert Black Money?' available at http://www.firstpost.com/business/demonetisation-nov-gold-imports-at-100-t-did-evaders-rush-to-convert-black-money-3135862.html, accessed on 23 January 2016.

Hindustan Times, 2016. 'No Limit on Holding Gold if It Matches Income Declaration: Govt', available at http://www.hindustantimes.com/india-news/no-limit-on-holding-gold-if-it-matches-income-declaration-govt/story-tN83lPEs4bbqYHeulGb4EN.html, accessed on 23 January 2016.

PIB (Press Information Bureau). 2016. 'Various Points Clarified with Respect to Gold Jewellery and Ornaments', available at http://pib.nic.in/newsite/PrintRelease.aspx?relid=154754, accessed on 23 January 2016.

Reddy, Y. V. 1996. 'Gold in the Indian Economic System', Address at the Gold Economic Conference organised by the World Gold Council at New Delhi on 28 November 1996, available at https://rbi.org.in/Scripts/BS_SpeechesView.aspx?Id=28, accessed on 9 February 2017

Reddy, Y. V. 1997. 'Gold Banking in India', Address at the World Gold Council Conference held in New Delhi on 2 August 1997, available at https://rbi.org.in/Scripts/BS_SpeechesView.aspx?Id=237, accessed on 9 February 2017.

The Economic Times. 2016. 'Crackdown on Black Money Puts Safe Boxes in Banks under Spotlight', available at http://economictimes.indiatimes.com/news/economy/policy/crackdown-on-black-money-puts-safe-boxes-in-banks-under-spotlight/articleshow/55628352.cms, accessed on 23 January 2016.

Annexures

— *Annexure I* —

Speech of the Prime Minister, 8 November 2016

My dear citizens

I hope you ended the festive season of Diwali with joy and new hope. Today, I will be speaking to you about some critical issues and important decisions. Today I want to make a special request to all of you. You may recall the economic situation in May 2014 when you entrusted us with an onerous responsibility. In the context of BRICS, it was being said that the "I" in BRICS was shaky. Since then, we had two years of severe drought. Yet, in the last two and a half years with the support of 125 crore Indians, India has become the "bright spot" in the global economy. It is not just we who are saying this; it is being stated by the International Monetary Fund and the World Bank.

In this effort for development, our motto has been 'Sab Ka Saath Sab Ka Vikas': We are with all citizens and for development of all citizens. This Government is dedicated to the poor. It will remain dedicated to them. In our fight against poverty, our main thrust has been to empower the poor, and make them active participants in the benefits of economic progress.

The Pradhan Mantri Jan Dhan Yojana,

- the Jan Suraksha Yojana,
- the Pradhan Mantri Mudra Yojana for small enterprises,
- the Stand-up India programme for Dalits, Adivasis and Women,
- the Pradhan Mantri Ujjwala Scheme for gas connections in the homes of the poor,
- the Pradhan Mantri Fasal Beema Yojana and Pradhan Mantri Krishi Sinchai Yojana to protect the income of farmers,
- the Soil Health Card Scheme to ensure the best possible yield from farmers' fields,

- and the e-NAM National Market Place scheme to ensure farmers get the right price for their produce

—these are all reflections of this approach.

In the past decades, the spectre of corruption and black money has grown. It has weakened the effort to remove poverty. On the one hand, we are now No. 1 in the rate of economic growth. But on the other hand, we were ranked close to one hundred in the global corruption perceptions ranking two years back. In spite of many steps taken, we have only been able to reach a ranking of seventy-six now. Of course, there is improvement. This shows the extent to which corruption and black money have spread their tentacles.

The evil of corruption has been spread by certain sections of society for their selfish interest. They have ignored the poor and cornered benefits. Some people have misused their office for personal gain. On the other hand, honest people have fought against this evil. Crores of common men and women have lived lives of integrity. We hear about poor auto-rickshaw drivers returning gold ornaments left in the vehicles to their rightful owners. We hear about taxi drivers who take pains to locate the owners of cell phones left behind. We hear of vegetable vendors who return excess money given by customers.

There comes a time in the history of a country's development when a need is felt for a strong and decisive step. For years, this country has felt that corruption, black money and terrorism are festering sores, holding us back in the race towards development.

Terrorism is a frightening threat. So many have lost their lives because of it. But have you ever thought about how these terrorists get their money? Enemies from across the border run their operations using fake currency notes. This has been going on for years. Many times, those using fake five hundred and thousand rupee notes have been caught and many such notes have been seized.

Brothers and sisters,

On the one hand is the problem of terrorism; on the other is the challenge posed by corruption and black money. We began our battle against corruption by setting up an SIT headed by a retired Supreme Court judge, immediately upon taking office. Since then

- a law was passed in 2015 for disclosure of foreign black money;

- agreements with many countries, including the USA, have been made to add provisions for sharing banking information;
- a strict law has come into force from August 2016 to curb benami transactions, which are used to deploy black money earned through corruption;
- a scheme was introduced for declaring black money after paying a stiff penalty;

My dear countrymen,

Through all these efforts, in the last two and a half years, we have brought into the open nearly 1 lakh 25 thousand crore rupees of black money belonging to the corrupt. Honest citizens want this fight against corruption, black money, benami property, terrorism and counterfeiting to continue. Which honest citizen would not be pained by reports of crores worth of currency notes stashed under the beds of government officers? Or by reports of cash found in gunny bags?

The magnitude of cash in circulation is directly linked to the level of corruption. Inflation becomes worse through the deployment of cash earned in corrupt ways. The poor have to bear the brunt of this. It has a direct effect on the purchasing power of the poor and the middle class. You may yourself have experienced when buying land or a house, that apart from the amount paid by cheque, a large amount is demanded in cash. This creates problems for an honest person in buying property. The misuse of cash has led to artificial increase in the cost of goods and services like houses, land, higher education, health care and so on.

High circulation of cash also strengthens the hawala trade which is directly connected to black money and illegal trade in weapons. Debate on the role of black money in elections has been going on for years.

Brothers and sisters,

To break the grip of corruption and black money, we have decided that the five hundred rupee and thousand rupee currency notes presently in use will no longer be legal tender from midnight tonight, that is 8th November 2016. This means that these notes will not be acceptable for transactions from midnight onwards. The five hundred and thousand rupee notes hoarded by anti-national and anti-social elements will become just worthless pieces of paper. The rights and the interests of honest, hard-working people will be fully protected. Let me assure you that notes of one hundred, fifty, twenty, ten, five, two and one rupee and all coins will remain legal tender and will not be affected.

This step will strengthen the hands of the common man in the fight against corruption, black money and fake currency. To minimise the difficulties of citizens in the coming days, several steps are being taken.

1. Persons holding old notes of five hundred or one thousand rupees can deposit these notes in their bank or post office accounts from 10th November till close of banking hours on 30th December 2016 without any limit.
2. Thus you will have 50 days to deposit your notes and there is no need for panic.
3. Your money will remain yours. You need have no worry on this point.
4. After depositing your money in your account, you can draw it when you need it.
5. Keeping in mind the supply of new notes, in the first few days, there will be a limit of ten thousand rupees per day and twenty thousand rupees per week. This limit will be increased in the coming days.
6. Apart from depositing your notes in your bank account, another facility will also be there.
7. For your immediate needs, you can go to any bank, head post office or sub post office, show your identity proof like Aadhaar card, voter card, ration card, passport, PAN card or other approved proofs, and exchange your old five hundred or thousand rupee notes for new notes.
8. From 10th November till 24th November the limit for such exchange will be four thousand rupees. From 25th November till 30th December, the limit will be increased.
9. There may be some who, for some reason, are not able to deposit their old five hundred or thousand rupee notes by 30th December 2016.
10. They can go to specified offices of the Reserve Bank of India up to 31st March 2017 and deposit the notes after submitting a declaration form.
11. On 9th November and in some places on 10th November also, ATMs will not work. In the first few days, there will be a limit of two thousand rupees per day per card.

12. This will be raised to four thousand rupees later.
13. Five hundred and thousand rupee notes will not be legal tender from midnight. However for humanitarian reasons, to reduce hardship to citizens, some special arrangements have been made for the first 72 hours, that is till midnight on 11th November.
14. During this period, government hospitals will continue to accept five hundred and thousand rupee notes for payment.
15. This is for the benefit of those families whose members may be unwell.
16. Pharmacies in government hospitals will also accept these notes for buying medicines with doctors' prescription.
17. For 72 hours, till midnight on 11th November, railway ticket booking counters, ticket counters of government buses and airline ticket counters at airports will accept the old notes for purchase of tickets. This is for the benefit of those who may be travelling at this time.
18. For 72 hours, five hundred and thousand rupee notes will be accepted also at
    - Petrol, diesel and CNG gas stations authorised by public sector oil companies
    - Consumer co-operative stores authorised by State or Central Government
    - Milk booths authorised by State governments
    - Crematoria and burial grounds.

    These outlets will have to keep proper records of stock and collections.
19. Arrangements will be made at international airports for arriving and departing passengers who have five hundred or thousand rupee notes of not more than five thousand rupees, to exchange them for new notes or other legal tender.
20. Foreign tourists will be able to exchange foreign currency or old notes of not more than Rs 5000 into legal tender.
21. One more thing I would like to mention, I want to stress that in this entire exercise, there is no restriction of any kind on non-cash payments by cheques, demand drafts, debit or credit cards and electronic fund transfer.

Brothers and sisters,

In spite of all these efforts there may be temporary hardships to be faced by honest citizens. Experience tells us that ordinary citizens are always ready to make sacrifices and face difficulties for the benefit of the nation. I see that spirit when a poor widow gives up her LPG subsidy, when a retired school teacher contributes his pension to the Swacch Bharat mission, when a poor Adivasi mother sells her goats to build a toilet, when a soldier contributes 57 thousand rupees to make his village clean. I have seen that the ordinary citizen has the determination to do anything, if it will lead to the country's progress.

So, in this fight against corruption, black money, fake notes and terrorism, in this movement for purifying our country, will our people not put up with difficulties for some days? I have full confidence that every citizen will stand up and participate in this 'mahayagna'. My dear countrymen, after the festivity of Diwali, now join the nation and extend your hand in this Imandaari ka Utsav, this Pramanikta ka Parv, this celebration of integrity, this festival of credibility.

I am sure that all political parties, all governments, social services organizations, the media and indeed all sections of the society will take part in this with enthusiasm and make it a success.

My dear countrymen,

Secrecy was essential for this action. It is only now, as I speak to you, that various agencies like banks, post offices, railways, hospitals and others are being informed. The Reserve Bank, banks and post offices have to make many arrangements at very short notice. Obviously, time will be needed. Therefore all banks will be closed to the public on 9th November. This may cause some hardship to you. I have full faith that banks and post offices will successfully carry out this great task of national importance. However, I appeal to all of you to help the banks and post offices to meet this challenge with poise and determination.

My dear citizens,

From time to time, based on currency needs, the Reserve Bank with the approval of the Central Government brings out new notes of higher value. In 2014, the Reserve Bank sent a recommendation for issue of five thousand and ten thousand rupee notes. After careful consideration, this was not accepted. Now as part of this exercise, RBI's recommendation to issue two thousand rupee notes has been accepted. New notes of five hundred rupees and two thousand rupees, with completely new design will be introduced. Based on past experience, the Reserve Bank will hereafter make arrangements to limit the share of high denomination notes in the total currency in circulation.

In a country's history, there come moments when every person feels he too should be part of that moment, that he too should make his contribution to the country's progress. Such moments come but rarely. Now, we again have an opportunity where every citizen can join this mahayajna against the ills of corruption, black money and fake notes. The more help you give in this campaign, the more successful it will be.

It has been a matter of concern for all of us that corruption and black money tend to be accepted as part of life. This type of thinking has afflicted our politics, our administration and our society like an infestation of termites. None of our public institutions is free from these termites.

Time and again, I have seen that when the average citizen has to choose between accepting dishonesty and bearing inconvenience, they always choose to put up with inconvenience. They will not support dishonesty.

Once again, let me invite you to make your contribution to this grand sacrifice for cleansing our country, just as you cleaned up your surroundings during Diwali.

Let us ignore the temporary hardship
Let us join this festival of integrity and credibility
Let us enable coming generations to live their lives with dignity
Let us fight corruption and black money
Let us ensure that the nation's wealth benefits the poor
Let us enable law-abiding citizens to get their due share.

I am confident in the 125 crore people of India and I am sure country will get success.

Thank you very much. Thanks a lot.

Namaskar.

Source: PMO website.

— *Annexure II* —

Gazette Notification on Demonetisation

Ministry of Finance
(Department of Economic Affairs)

Notification
New Delhi, the 8th November, 2016

S.O. 3407(E).—Whereas, the Central Board of Directors of the Reserve Bank of India (hereinafter referred to as the Board) has recommended that bank notes of denominations of the existing series of the value of five hundred rupees and one thousand rupees (hereinafter referred to as specified bank notes) shall be ceased to be legal tender;

And whereas, it has been found that fake currency notes of the specified bank notes have been largely in circulation and it has been found to be difficult to easily identify genuine bank notes from the fake ones and that the use of fake currency notes is causing adverse effect to the economy of the country;

And whereas, it has been found that high denomination bank notes are used for storage of unaccounted wealth as has been evident from the large cash recoveries made by law enforcement agencies;

And whereas, it has also been found that fake currency is being used for financing subversive activities such as drug trafficking and terrorism, causing damage to the economy and security of the country and the Central Government after due consideration has decided to implement the recommendations of the Board;

Now, therefore, in exercise of the powers conferred by sub-section (2) of section 26 of the Reserve Bank of

India Act, 1934 (2 of 1934) (hereinafter referred to as the said Act), the Central Government hereby declares that the specified bank notes shall cease to be legal tender with effect from the 9th November, 2016 to the extent specified below,

namely:—

1. (1) Every banking company defined under the Banking Regulation Act, 1949 (10 of 1949) and every Government Treasury shall complete and forward a return showing the details of specified bank notes held by it at the close of business as on the 8th November, 2016, not later than 13:00 hours on the 10th November, 2016 to the designated Regional Office of the Reserve Bank of India (hereinafter referred to as the Reserve Bank) in the format specified by it.
   (2) Immediately after forwarding the return referred to in sub-paragraph (1), the specified bank notes shall be remitted to the linked or nearest currency chest, or the branch or office of the Reserve Bank, for credit to their accounts.
2. The specified bank notes held by a person other than a banking company referred to in sub-paragraph (1) of paragraph 1 or Government Treasury may be exchanged at any Issue Office of the Reserve Bank or any branch of public sector banks, private sector banks, foreign banks, Regional Rural Banks, Urban Cooperative Banks and State Cooperative Banks for a period up to and including the 30th December, 2016, subject to the following conditions, namely:—
   (i) the specified bank notes of aggregate value of Rs 4,000/- or below may be exchanged for any denomination of bank notes having legal tender character, with a requisition slip in the format specified by the Reserve Bank and proof of identity;
   (ii) the limit of Rs 4,000/- for exchanging specified bank notes shall be reviewed after fifteen days from the date of commencement of this notification and appropriate orders may be issued, where necessary;
   (iii) there shall not be any limit on the quantity or value of the specified bank notes to be credited to the account maintained with the bank by a person, where the specified bank notes are tendered; however, where compliance with

extant Know Your Customer (KYC) norms is not complete in an account, the maximum value of specified bank notes as may be deposited shall be Rs 50,000/-;

(iv) the equivalent value of specified bank notes tendered may be credited to an account maintained by the tenderer at any bank in accordance with standard banking procedure and on production of valid proof of Identity;

(v) the equivalent value of specified bank notes tendered may be credited to a third party account, provided specific authorisation therefor accorded by the third party is presented to the bank, following standard banking procedure and on production of valid proof of identity of the person actually tendering;

(vi) cash withdrawal from a bank account over the counter shall be restricted to Rs 10,000/- per day subject to an overall limit of Rs 20,000/- a week from the date of commencement of this notification until the end of business hours on 24th November, 2016, after which these limits shall be reviewed;

(vii) there shall be no restriction on the use of any non-cash method of operating the account of a person including cheques, demand drafts, credit or debit cards, mobile wallets and electronic fund transfer mechanisms or the like;

(viii) withdrawal from Automatic Teller Machines (hereinafter referred to as ATMs) shall be restricted to Rs 2,000 per day per card up to 18th November, 2016 and the limit shall be raised to Rs 4,000 per day per card from 19th November, 2016;

(ix) any person who is unable to exchange or deposit the specified bank notes in their bank accounts on or before the 30th December, 2016, shall be given an opportunity to do so at specified offices of the Reserve Bank or such other facility until a later date as may be specified by it.

3. (1) Every banking company and every Government Treasury referred to in sub-paragraph (1) of paragraph 1 shall be closed for the transaction of all business on 9th November, 2016, except the preparation for implementing this scheme and remittance of the specified bank notes to nearby

currency chests or the branches or offices of the Reserve Bank and receipt of bank notes having legal tender character.

(2) All ATMs, Cash Deposit Machines, Cash Recyclers and any other machine used for receipt and payment of cash shall be shut on 9th and 10th November, 2016.

(3) Every bank referred to in sub-paragraph (1) of paragraph 1 shall recall the specified bank notes from ATMs and replace them with bank notes having legal tender character prior to reactivation of the machines on 11th November,2016.

(4) The sponsor banks of White Label ATMs shall be responsible to recall the specified bank notes from the White Label ATMs and replacing the same with bank notes having legal tender character prior to reactivation of the machines on 11th November, 2016.

(5) All banks referred to in sub-paragraph (1) of paragraph 1 shall ensure that their ATMs and White Label ATMs shall dispense bank notes of denomination of Rs 100 or Rs 50, until further instructions from the Reserve Bank.

(6) The banking company referred to in sub-paragraph (1) of paragraph 1 and Government Treasuries shall resume their normal transactions from 10th November, 2016.

4. Every banking company referred to sub-paragraph (1) of paragraph 1, shall at the close of business of each day starting from 10th November, 2016, submit to the Reserve Bank, a statement showing the details of specified bank notes exchanged by it in such format as may be specified by the Reserve Bank.

[F.No.10/03/2016-Cy.I]
Dr. Saurabh Garg, Jt. Secy.

Source: From *The Gazette of India: Extraordinary* [Part II—Sec. 3(ii)], No. 2652 New Delhi, Tuesday, November 8, 2016/Kartika 17, 1938.

— Annexure III —

Speech of Dr. Manmohan Singh in the Rajya Sabha

I rise to highlight some of the problems that have risen after the decision to demonetise Rs 500 and Rs 1000 currency notes.

Prime Minister has been arguing that this is the way to curb black money, to prevent growth of forfeiture currency notes and also to help in control of terrorist finance activities. I do not disagree with these objectives. But I do want to point out this that in the process of demonetisation monumental mismanagement has been undertaken about which today there is no two opinions in the country as a whole. Even those who say that this measure will do harm or cause distress in the short term but be in the interests of the country in the long run should be reminded of what John Keynes said once," In the long run all of us are dead."

And therefore, it is important to take note of grievances of the ordinary people who have suffered as a result of this imposition on the country overnight by the Prime Minister. And I say so with all responsibilities, that we do not know what will be the final outcome.

Prime Minister has said that we should wait for 50 days. Well 50 days is a short period. But for those who are poor and from the deprived sections of the society even 50 days torture can bring about disastrous effects. And that's why about 60 to 65 people have lost their lives, maybe more. And what has been done can weaken and erode our people's confidence in the currency system and in the banking system.

I would like to know from the Prime Minister the name of any country he may think of where people have deposited their money in the banks but they are not allowed to withdraw their money. This alone, I think, is enough to condemn what has been done in the name of greater good of the people of the country.

And Sir, I would further like to point out that in my opinion that the way the scheme has been implemented will hurt agricultural growth in our country, will hurt small industry, will hurt all those people who are in the informal sector of the economy. And my own feeling is that the national income, that is the GDP, can decline by about 2 per cent as a result of what has been done. This is an underestimate, not an overestimate. Therefore, I feel that the Prime Minister must come up with some constructive proposal on how we can implement this scheme and at the same time prevent this distress that has been caused to the common people.

It is no good that everyday the banking system comes with modification of the rules, the conditions under which the people can withdraw money. That reflects very poorly on the Prime Minister's office, on the Finance Minister's office and on the Reserve Bank of India. I am very sorry that the Reserve Bank of India has been exposed to this sort of criticism which I think is fully justified.

I, therefore, would not like to say much more than this. I urge upon the Prime Minister to find practical, pragmatic ways and means to relieve the distress of the people who happen to be a great majority. After all, 90 per cent of our people work in the informal sector, 55 per cent of our workers in agriculture are reeling in distress. The cooperative banking system which serves large number of people in the rural areas is non-functional and has been prevented from handling cash. So, in all these measures convince me that the way this scheme has been implemented is a monumental management failure, and in fact, it is a case of organised loot, legalised plunder of the common people.

With these words, sir, I conclude. It is not my intention to pick holes in what one side does or another side does. But I sincerely hope that the Prime Minister will view that this late hour will help us to find practical, pragmatic ways and means to provide relief to the suffering of the people of this country. Thank you.

Source: Dr. Manmohan Singh's speech; Rajya Sabha website.

— *Annexure IV* —

Extract from 2012 White Paper

2.2 Factors leading to generation of Black Economy

2.2.1 Black money arising from illegal activities such as crime and corruption has an underlying anti-social element. The 'criminal' component of black money may include proceeds from a range of activities including racketeering, trafficking in counterfeit and contraband goods, smuggling, production and trade of narcotics, forgery, illegal mining, illegal felling of forests, illicit liquor trade, robbery, kidnapping, human trafficking, sexual exploitation and prostitution, cheating and financial fraud, embezzlement, drug money, bank frauds, and illegal trade in arms. Some of these offences are included in the schedule of the Prevention of Money Laundering Act 2002. The 'corrupt' component of such money could stem from bribery and theft by those holding public office—such as by grant of business, leakages from government social spending programmes, speed money to circumvent or fast-track procedures, black marketing of price-controlled services, and altering land use regularizing unauthorized construction. All these activities are illegal per se and a result of human greed combined with declining societal values and inability of the state to prevent them. Factors leading to their generation are both social and administrative.

2.2.2 These illegal activities are punishable under various Acts of the central and state governments which are administered by various law enforcement agencies. Effective implementation of these Acts is the responsibility of both state and central governments.

2.2.3 Significant amount of black money, however, is generated through legally permissible economic activities, which are not accounted for and disclosed or reported to the public authorities as per the law or regulations, thereby converting such income into black money. The failure to report or disclose such activities or income may be with the objective of evading taxes or avoiding the cost of compliance related to such reporting or disclosure. It may also be the result of non-compliance with some other law. For example, a factory owner may under-report production on account of theft of electricity which in turn leads to evasion of taxes. Generally, a high burden of taxation, either actual or perceived, provides a strong temptation to evade taxes and generate black money. Sometimes the procedural regulations can be such that complying with them may increase the probability of further scrutiny and thereby the incidence of the burden of compliance, creating a perverse incentive not to report at all and remain outside the reported and accounted proportion of the economy. Culture and social practices may also play a vital role in deciding the preferences of citizens between tax compliance and black money generation. In a society where tax evasion and under-reporting of activities and income is perceived to be very common or the norm, such activities may be considered acceptable and honest tax compliance and paying one's due share to the public fund may not be considered a virtue. Studies indicate that countries with relatively poor implementation of regulations tend to have a higher share of unaccounted economy, whereas countries with properly implemented regulations and sound deterrence have smaller 'black' economies.

2.2.4 Thus the fight against generation and accumulation of black money is likely to be far more complex, requiring stronger intervention of the state, in developing countries like India than in developed countries. It needs a stronger legal framework, commensurate administrative measures, and a very strong resolve to fight the menace. It also calls for political consensus as well as patience and perseverance.

2.3 Generating Black Money by Manipulation of Accounts

2.3.1 There can be two different modi operandi involved in the generation of black money. The first is the crude approach of not declaring or reporting the whole of the income or the activities leading to it. This is the likely approach in all cases of criminal, illegal, and impermissible activities. The sophistications in such an approach mostly get introduced subsequently for the purpose of laundering the money so generated with the objective of making it accountable and converting it into legitimate reported wealth that can be openly possessed and used.

2.3.2 The same approach of not declaring or reporting activities and the income generated therefrom may also be followed in cases of failure to comply with regulatory obligations or tax evasion on income from legitimate activities. However, complete evasion or non-compliance may make such incomes vulnerable to detection by authorities and lead to consequent adverse outcomes for the generator. Thus a more sophisticated approach for generation of this kind of black money is often preferred, involving manipulation of financial records and accounting.

2.3.3 The best way of classifying and understanding the various ways and means adopted by taxpayers for the generation of black money would be the financial statement approach, elaborating different means by which the accounts prepared for reporting and presenting before the authorities are manipulated to misrepresent and underdisclose income, thereby generating unaccounted, undeclared, and unreported income that amounts to black money.

2.3.4 Any transaction entered into by the taxpayer must be reported in books of account which are summarised at the end of the year in the form of financial statements. The financial statements basically comprise statement of income and expenditure which is called by different names such as 'Profit and Loss Account' or 'Income and Expenditure Account' and statement of assets and liabilities which is called 'Balance Sheet' or 'Statement of Affairs'. Tax evasion involves misreporting or non-reporting of the transactions in the books of account. Different kinds of manipulations of financial statements resulting in tax evasion and the generation of black money are summarised in Figure 2.1 and and some of these are elaborated in the following paragraphs.

2.3.5 Out of Book Transactions: This is one of the simplest and most widely adopted methods of tax evasion and generation of black money. Transactions that may result in taxation of receipts or income are not entered in the books of account by the taxpayer. The taxpayer either does not maintain books of account or maintains two sets or records partial receipts only. This mode is generally prevalent among the small grocery shops, unskilled or semi-skilled service providers, etc.

2.3.6 Parallel Books of Accounts: This is a practice usually adopted by those who are obliged under the law or due to business needs to maintain books of account. In order to evade reporting activities or the income generated from them, they may resort to maintaining two sets of books of account—one for their own consumption with the objective of managing their business and the other one for the regulatory and tax authorities such as the Income Tax Department, Sales Tax Department, and Excise and Customs Department. The second set of books of account, which is maintained for the purpose

FIGURE 2.1: Manipulations of Accounts for Tax Evasion

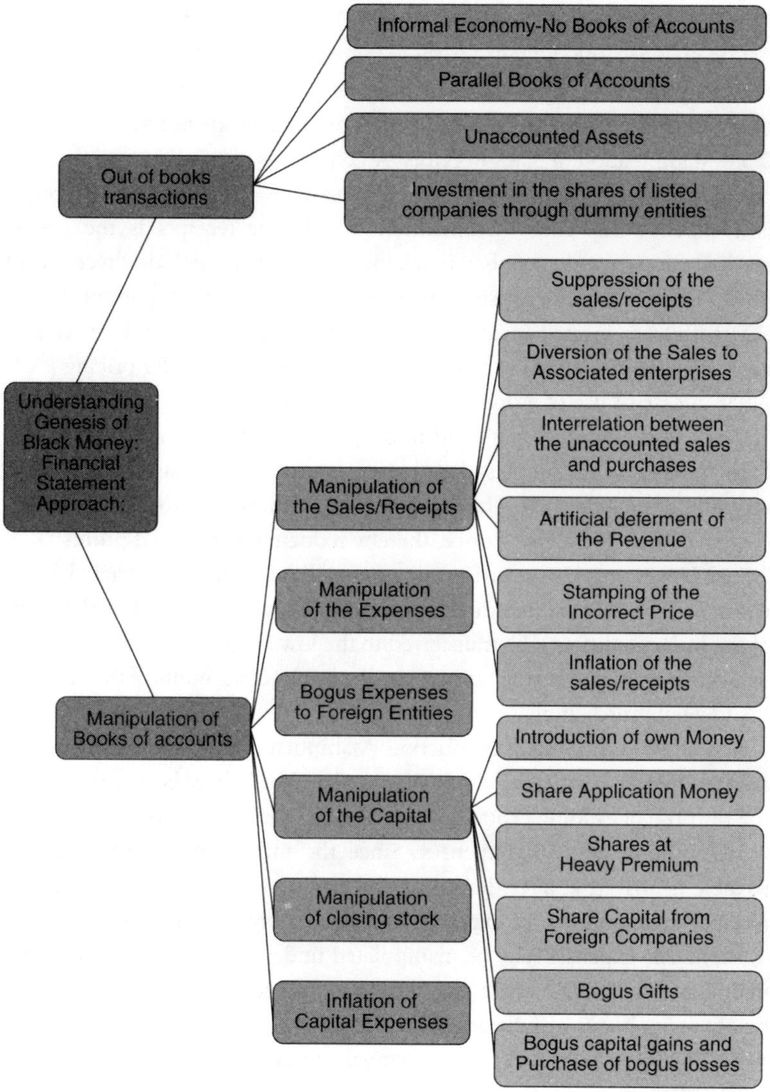

of satisfying the legal and regulatory obligations of reporting to different authorities, may be manipulated by omitting receipts or falsely inflating expenses, for the purpose of evading taxes or other regulatory requirements.

2.3.7 Manipulation of Books of Account: When books of accounts are required to be maintained by taxpayers under different laws, like the Companies Act 1956, the Banking Regulation Act, and the Income Tax Act, it may become difficult for these taxpayers to indulge in out of books transactions or to maintain parallel books of accounts. Such parties may resort to manipulation of the books of accounts to evade taxes.

2.3.8 Manipulation of Sales/Receipts: A taxpayer is required to pay taxes on profit or income which is the difference between sale proceeds or receipts and expenditure. Thus manipulation of sales or receipts is the easiest method of tax evasion. Other innovative means may include diversion of sales to associated enterprises, which may become more important if such enterprises are located in different tax jurisdictions and thereby may also give rise to issues related to international taxation and transfer pricing.

2.3.9 In case of use of a dummy / associated entity, there can be a plethora of possible arrangements entered into by such entities to aid generation of black money. In its simplest form, the associate entity may not report its activities or income at all. The main entity may show sales to such a dummy / associate entity at a lower price, thereby reducing its reported profits.

2.3.10 More complex scenarios can emerge if the dummy/ associated entity is situated in a low tax jurisdiction having very low tax rates. Thus the profit of the Indian entity will be transferred to the low tax jurisdiction and money will be accumulated by the taxpayer in the books of accounts of the entity in the low tax jurisdiction.

2.3.11 Under-reporting of Production: Manipulation of production figure is another means of artificially reducing tax liability. It may be resorted to for the purpose of evading central excise, sales tax, or income tax.

2.3.12 Manipulation of Expenses: Since the income on which taxes are payable is arrived at after deducting the expenses of the business from the receipts, manipulation of expenses is a commonly adopted method of tax evasion. The expenses may be manipulated under different heads and result in under-reporting of income. It may involve inflation of expenses, sometimes by obtaining bogus or inflated invoices from the so called 'bill masters', who make bogus vouchers and charge nominal commission for this facility.

2.3.13 Any number of more sophisticated versions of manipulation of expenses can also be resorted to by those intending to generate black money. Sometimes it can also involve 'hawala' operators, who operate shell entities in the form of proprietorship firms, partnership firms, companies, and trusts.

These operators may accept cheques for payments claimed as expense and return cash after charging some commission. There have been instances of claims of bogus expenses to foreign entities. The payments can be shown to foreign entities in the form of advertisement and marketing expenses or commission for purchases or sales. The funds may be remitted to the account of the foreign taxpayer and the money can either be withdrawn in cash or remitted back to India in the form of non-taxable receipts. Such money may also be accumulated in the form of unaccounted assets of the Indian taxpayer abroad.

2.3.14 Other Manipulations of Accounts: Besides inflation of purchase / raw material cost, expenses like labour charges, entertainment expenses, and commission can be inflated or falsely booked to reduce profits. In these cases, bogus bills may be prepared to show inflated expenses in the books.

2.3.15 Manipulation by Way of International Transactions through Associate Enterprises: Another way of manipulating accounted profits and taxes payable thereon may involve using associated enterprises in low tax jurisdictions through which goods or other material may be passed on to the concern. Inter-corporate transactions between these associate enterprises belonging to the same group or owned and controlled by the same set of parties may be arranged and manipulated in a way that leads to evasion of taxes. This can often be achieved by arrangements that shift taxable income to the low tax jurisdictions or tax havens, and may lead to accumulation of black money earned from within India to another country.

2.3.16 Manipulation of Capital: The statement of affairs or balance sheet of the taxpayer contains details of assets, liabilities, and capital. The capital of the taxpayer is the accumulated wealth which is invested in the form of assets or as working capital of the business. Manipulation of capital can be one of the ways of laundering and introduction of black money in books of accounts.

2.3.17 Manipulation of Closing Stock: Suppression of closing stock both in terms of quality and value is one of the most common methods of understating profit. More sophisticated versions of such practice may include omission of goods in transit paid for and debited to purchases, or omission of goods sent to the customer for approval. A more common approach is undervaluation of inventory (stock of unsold goods), which means that while the expenses are being accounted for in the books, the value being added is not accounted for, thereby artificially reducing the profits.

2.3.18 Manipulation of Capital Expenses: Over-invoicing plant and equipment or any capital asset is an approach adopted to claim higher depreciation and thereby reduce the profit of the business. As already stated, increase in capital can also be a means of enabling the businessman to borrow more funds from banks or raise capital from the market. It has been seen that such measures are sometimes resorted to at the time of bringing out a capital issue. At the same time, under-invoiced investments, indicating entry of undeclared wealth, may imply introduction of black money.

2.4 Generation of Black money in Some Vulnerable Sections of the Economy

2.4.1 While the source of generation of black money may lie in any sphere of economic activity, there are certain sectors of the economy or activities, which are more vulnerable to this menace. These include real estate, the bullion and jewellery market, financial markets, public procurement, non-profit organizations, external trade, international transactions involving tax havens, and the informal service sector.

2.4.2 Land and Real Estate Transactions: Due to rising prices of real estate, the tax incidence applicable on real estate transactions in the form of stamp duty and capital gains tax can create incentives for tax evasion through under-reporting of transaction price. This can lead to both generation and investment of black money. The buyer has the option of investing his black money by paying cash in addition to the documented sale consideration. This also leads to generation of black money in the hands of the recipient. A more sophisticated form occasionally resorted to consists of cash for the purchase of transferable development rights (TDR)[1].

2.4.3 Bullion and Jewellery Transactions: Cash sales in the gold and jewellery trade are quite common and serve two purposes. The purchase allows the buyer the option of converting black money into gold and bullion, while it gives the trader the option of keeping his unaccounted wealth in the form of stock, not disclosed in the books or valued at less than market price.

2.4.4 Financial Market Transactions: Financial market transactions can involve black money in different forms. Initial public offers (IPOs) offering equity shares to the public at large are also vulnerable to various manipulations that can generate black money for the promoters or operators. Rigging of

[1] TDRs are rights for construction beyond the usual limits, which can be transferred by the owner. These rights can be made available in lieu of area or land surrendered by the owner.

markets by the market operators is one such means. This may involve use of shell companies and more sophisticated versions of such manipulation may involve offshore companies or investors in foreign tax jurisdictions who invest in shares offered by the IPO and through manipulated trading escalate their price artificially, only to offload them later at the cost of ordinary investors.

2.4.5 Public Procurement: Public procurement has grown phenomenally over the years—in volume, scale, and variety as well as complexity. It often includes sophisticated and hi-tech items, complex works, and a wide range of services. An OECD (Organisation for Economic Cooperation and Development) estimate puts the figure for public procurement in India at 30 per cent of the GDP whereas a WTO (World Trade Organisation) estimate puts this figure at 20 per cent of the GDP.[2] The Competition Commission of India had estimated in a paper that the annual public sector procurement in India would be of the order of ` 8 lakh crore while a rough estimation of direct government procurement is between ` 2.5 and 3 lakh crore. This puts the total public procurement figure for India at around ` 10 to 11 lakh crore per year.[3]

2.4.6 Non-profit Sector: Taxation laws allow certain privileges and incentives for promoting charitable activities. Misuse of such benefits and manipulations through entities claimed to be constituted for non-profit motive are among possible sources of generation of black money. Such misuse has also been highlighted by the Financial Action Task Force (FATF), an intergovernmental body which develops and promotes policies to protect the global financial system against money laundering and financing of terrorism. A Non-profit Organisation (NPO) Sector Assessment Committee constituted under the Ministry of Finance has reviewed the existing control and legal mechanisms for the NPO sector and suggested various measures for improvement.

2.4.7 Informal Sector and Cash Economy: The issue of black money is related to the magnitude of cash transactions in the informal economy. The demand for currency is determined by a number of factors such as income, price levels, and opportunity cost of holding currency. Factors like dependence on agriculture, existence of a large informal sector, and insufficient banking

[2] Ref: Para 1.5 of the Report of the Committee on Public Procurement, 6 June 2011.

[3] Ibid.

infrastructure with large un-banked and under-banked areas contribute to the large cash economy in India.

2.4.8 External trade and Transfer Pricing: More than 60 per cent[4] of global trade is carried out between associated enterprises of multinational enterprises (MNEs). Since allocation of costs and overheads and fixing of price of product/services are highly subjective, MNEs enjoy considerable discretion in allocating costs and prices to particular products/services and geographical jurisdictions. Such discretion enables them to transfer profit/income to no tax or low tax jurisdictions. Differing tax rates in different tax jurisdictions can create perverse incentives for corporations to shift taxable income from jurisdictions with relatively high tax rates to jurisdictions with relatively low tax rates as a means of minimising their tax liability. For example, a foreign parent company could use internal 'transfer prices' for overstating the value of goods and services that it exports to its foreign affiliate in order to shift taxable income from the operations of the affiliate in a high tax jurisdiction to its operations in a low-tax jurisdiction. Similarly, the foreign affiliate might understate the value of goods and services that it exports to the parent company in order to shift taxable income from its high tax jurisdiction to the low tax jurisdiction of its parent. Both of these strategies would shift the company's profits to the low tax jurisdiction and, in so doing; reduce its worldwide tax payments. In this context transfer pricing has emerged as the biggest tool for generation and transfer of black money. In recent years, after the 9/11 incident in the USA due to intense scrutiny of banking transactions, enhanced security checks at airports and ports, and relaxation of exchange controls, transfer of money through hawala has reduced significantly but now transfer pricing is now being extensively used to transfer income/profit and avoid taxes at will across countries. Also, with the relaxation of exchange controls and liberalisation of banking channels, the popularity of the hawala system for legitimate transfers has reduced substantially. The increasing pressure on financial operators and banks to report cash transactions has also helped in curbing hawala transactions. Tax evasion through transfer pricing is largely invisible to the public and difficult and expensive for tax officers to detect. Christianaid[5] estimates that

[4] Christianaid, Death and Taxes: The Truth of Tax Dodging, March 2009.

[5] Ibid.

developing countries may be losing over US$160billion of tax revenues a year, primarily through transfer pricing strategies.

2.4.9 The illicit money transferred outside India may come back to India through various methods such as hawala, mispricing, foreign direct investment (FDI) through beneficial tax jurisdictions, raising of capital by Indian companies through global depository receipts (GDRs), and investment in Indian stock markets through participatory notes. It is possible that a large amount of money transferred outside India might actually have returned through these means.

2.4.10 Trade-based Money Laundering (TBML): The FATF defines TBML as the process of disguising the proceeds of crime and moving value through the use of trade transactions in an attempt at legitimising their illicit origins. Factors that facilitate such manipulation include the enormous volume of international trade flow, the complexity associated with financing arrangements and currency exchanges as well as limited recourse to verification procedures between countries.

2.4.11 Tax Havens: The term 'tax haven' has been widely used since the 1950s. However, there is no precise definition of the term. The OECD initially defined tax havens as being characterised by no or very low taxes, lack of effective exchange of information, and lack of transparency about substantial activities. It listed 35 countries/ jurisdictions as tax havens in the year 2000. The list has changed over time as more tax havens have made agreements to share information.

2.4.12 Offshore Financial Centres: Some of the old tax havens have adopted the more benign designation of 'offshore financial centre' (OFC) and tend to describe themselves as financial centres specializing in non-residential financial transactions. However, with their array of secrecy provisions that lack regulation, the zero or near zero taxation imposed by them, and lack of adequate capital controls, they are logical extensions of the traditional tax havens. The IMF has defined OFCs as centers where the bulk of financial sector transactions on both sides of the balance sheet are with individuals or companies that are not residents, where the transactions are initiated elsewhere, and where the majority of the institutions involved are controlled by non-residents. Thus, many OFCs have the following characteristics:

1. Jurisdictions that have financial institutions engaged primarily in business with non-residents;

2. Financial systems with external assets and liabilities out of proportion to domestic financial intermediation designed to finance domestic economic; and
3. More popularly, centers which provide some or all of the following opportunities: low or zero taxation; moderate or light financial regulation; banking secrecy and anonymity.

International organizations including the BIS and IMF began to use the term OFC in a more restrictive manner to describe financial services that were evolving in tax havens.

2.4.13 Investment through Innovative Derivative Instruments: With increasing sophistication of derivative instruments, new opportunities for investing and making profits without being subjected to taxes and regulations are also opening up. Such innovative means can also be misused by unscrupulous parties to generate unaccounted income. Some such instruments like participatory notes may not be adequately covered by regulatory mechanisms and their oversight and hence have potential for misuse.

Box: Participatory Notes

A Participatory Note (PN) is a derivative instrument issued in foreign jurisdictions, by a Foreign Institutional Investor (FII) / its sub-accounts or one of its associates, against underlying Indian securities. PNs are popular among foreign investors since they allow these investors to earn returns on investment in the Indian market without undergoing the significant cost and time implications of directly investing in India. These instruments are traded overseas outside the direct purview of SEBI surveillance thereby raising many apprehensions about the beneficial ownership and the nature of funds invested in these instruments. Concerns have been raised that some of the money coming into the market via PNs could be the unaccounted wealth camouflaged under the guise of FII investment. SEBI has been taking measures to ensure that PNs are not used as conduits for black money or terrorist funding.

Source: 'Black Money: White Paper 2012' (Ministry of Finance), pp. 2–9, Box from p. 9.

Index